O's
Little Guide to Finding Your True Purpose

O's

Little Guide to Finding Your True Purpose

The Editors of *O, The Oprah Magazine*

FLATIRON
BOOKS
NEW YORK

www.flatironbooks.com

All material included in this book was previously published, in slightly
different form, in *O, The Oprah Magazine*. *O, The Oprah Magazine* is a
registered trademark of Harpo Print, LLC.

"It's All About What You Do With Your Breakthrough" was first published in
O, The Oprah Magazine, © 2013 by Martha Beck. "Take a Flying Leap"
(now titled "Faith, Hope, and Sasquatch") was first published in
O, The Oprah Magazine, © 2014 by Martha Beck.

The Library of Congress Cataloging-in-Publication Data
is available upon request.

ISBN 978-1-250-06858-3 (hardcover)
ISBN 978-1-250-06859-0 (e-book)

Our books may be purchased in bulk for promotional, educational,
or business use. Please contact your local bookseller or the Macmillan
Corporate and Premium Sales Department at (800) 221-7945, extension 5442,
or by e-mail at MacmillanSpecialMarkets@macmillan.com.

First Edition: October 2015

10 9 8 7 6 5 4 3 2 1

We're all called. If you're here breathing, you have a contribution to make to our human community. The real work of your life is to figure out your function—your part in the whole—as soon as possible, and then get about the business of fulfilling it as only you can.

—OPRAH WINFREY

Contents

Stirrings

Sometimes you hear a voice through the door
calling you. . . . This turning toward what you
deeply love saves you.

—RUMI

"This Is It, My Pet Pachooch!"

Bonnie Friedman

I used to yearn for a wake-up call. I thought often about an acquaintance who took a skydiving class; when her parachute didn't open, she fell more than a mile, crashing into a field. Miraculously, she lived. And as soon as her bones healed, she changed her entire life: divorced her husband, moved with her children to a house down the road, and let herself pursue what she really wanted. Of course, I didn't want the mile-long fall (or the divorce), but I did want this woman's visceral understanding that life is short and mustn't be wasted.

Even after I was struck by a car and sent flying four feet through the air, though, I wasn't shocked into transformation. I picked myself up, limped home, and continued to ignore a certain unhappiness in my marriage. I doggedly did my work and didn't confront problems.

A few years later, when my sister, who had been ill for decades with multiple sclerosis, passed away, I felt surprisingly little: I'd been saying good-bye to her for a long, long time.

But at the funeral home something happened. "Come here," the rabbi said, drawing my family into a side room. My glance fell on a simple pine box. *Naturally, there are coffins in funeral homes*, I thought—then realized it must be Anita's. It was so small, considering the large woman she'd become. So bare. That's all there is, it seemed to say. My heart flew out of me—oh, Anita! I suddenly missed the girl she'd been, the energetic hiker who sang Girl Scout songs and sipped Tab, who folded newspapers into admirals' hats so we could pretend to be adventurers. I even missed the wheelchair-bound woman who loved chocolate cake although someone had to feed it to her.

At the cemetery, in accordance with Jewish tradition, my father and brothers threw spades full of dirt onto the coffin—I demurred—and then the workmen filled the grave. It struck me as barbaric and mind-boggling to stand there while they actually buried Anita.

In the car going home, I sat beside my mother. "Life is a dream," she said. "My mother used to tell me that."

A mourning candle marked with a Jewish star flickered on my stove. As the days passed, I wondered if it was possible to return to the way I'd lived: drifting. I recalled how once, when Anita was already housebound, I'd asked what she was up to. She told me she'd just ordered a box of pens with the inscription *This is the day which the Lord has made. Rejoice and be glad in it.*

At the end of seven days, Orthodox Jews blow the candle out. For me, it felt like blowing out Anita's own soul, like releasing her to her new world and being expelled back to the land of the living. I took a slow walk around my Brooklyn block, and saw for the first time that even the street of throbbing, filthy diesel trucks held something sacred.

Ordinary life subsumed me after that, but only up to a point. Soon I sat my husband down and told him about the hollow places in our marriage—and our relationship gained energy; the life force flowed back in. I became more nurturing of my writing students and made it a higher priority to spend time with my parents.

What a relief to hear a wake-up call at last! I only wish

it hadn't taken the loss of my sister to rouse me. How much better to discover life's evanescence without the parachute failure or other calamity. Why wait for a near-death experience when life itself is a near-death experience? I wish someone had told me: You're allowed to hear the call even if the crisis happened to someone else. Life is always a risk, never a possession. Anita, who contemplated ultimate things, could have told me that. *Baby,* I can hear her say, *when it's over, it's over. This is it, my pet pachooch!* Better live in a way that inspires rejoicing.

"Our Irrecoverable Time"
Edwidge Danticat

It was one of the longest trips of my life. On the first leg of
the three-plane jaunt, the flight was delayed two hours,
leaving me with a mere ten minutes to dash to the second
plane. When I arrived at the third airport, two people ran
through the security checkpoint, resulting in the airport's
being shut down for hours. As I boarded the final plane, a
noisy propper, I hit my forehead so hard that I nearly passed
out, acquiring a fist-sized bump in the process. The worst
part of the trip, however, was that I didn't want to be on it.
An acquaintance had asked me to give a reading at her
school during an extremely busy time of the year, and to
make her happy, I had said yes.

A week before the trip, I called the school to check on
the travel arrangements and was told that I was expected

to make them myself and would be reimbursed later. I was tempted to book a first-class ticket on a first-rate airline, but because my acquaintance's school was low on funds, I got a discount ticket on the Internet, which sent me on that patchwork of flights.

When I finally reached her city, I was hungry and exhausted. Still, I proceeded to make small talk with my hostess on the hour-long car ride to my hotel. She was very cheerful, and between questions about everything from the color of my childhood house to my college English courses, she laid out the next day's heavy schedule of morning assemblies and afternoon classroom visits—which had not been part of our original agreement.

Not wanting to appear disagreeable, I bit my tongue and whispered, "Fine." Meanwhile I could feel the bump on my forehead growing bigger and bigger, like Pinocchio's nose rising after he told a lie.

When I arrived at the hotel, in order to bury my well-concealed frustration, I consumed a total of fifteen chocolate hearts, which had been decoratively placed around the room. The next day, however, the chocolate did nothing to sweeten my disposition or to make the bump on my forehead, which overnight had turned black and blue, go away. I did the best I could to conceal the swelling with makeup, but by the time I left the hotel room, what I often jokingly refer to as my wide and ample "four-head" was more like a "five-head." Nevertheless, I addressed the morning assemblies and then trudged through the back-to-back afternoon classes, praying I wouldn't faint from exhaustion or lose my voice.

The truth is, had I really wanted to be on this trip, I would have happily brushed off the consecutive pre-sentations and my aching head as yet another series of challenges to be overcome in my constant book-related travels. However, since I was putting myself through this particular experience more out of obligation than desire, I felt doubly abused, by both this person and myself. There were so many other things I could have been doing. I could have been writing. I could have been sleeping. I could have been lunching with my beloved. I could have been play-ing with my niece and nephew. I could have been consol-ing a dear friend who had recently lost her mother.

On the plane back, I got a chance to open a book that a friend who knew my tendency to over-please had given me, *The Early Journals and Letters of Fanny Burney*, an eighteenth-century novelist and letter writer. My friend had highlighted several sections, and in a rare moment's respite from the stomach-churning turbulence, I spotted these lines: "This perpetual round of constrained civilities to persons quite indifferent to us, is the most provoking and tiresome thing in the world . . . 'Tis a most shocking and unworthy way of spending our precious and irrecoverable time."

I now have that passage and the memory of the bump on my forehead to remind me. The next time I do any favor, large or small, I will have to be almost thrilled to death about it. Otherwise I will stay home and eat my own chocolates.

Illuminations

Marianne Williamson

Every woman's life is different, but there are fundamental ways in which we are all the same. For all our different dramas, we each struggle to give birth to our higher selves. Whether we are young or old, whether our dramas are public or private, we are always evolving toward either a smaller and more fearful self or a larger and more loving self. The effort to be rooted in love is the effort to grow.

The Beginning

Lorene Cary

The week after my first daughter was born I took her to visit my grandparents. When I was a girl, I spent weekends with them; now a married woman, I still drove over the Delaware River from Philadelphia to New Jersey to have an afternoon and evening with them and my father once a week. Like phone calls in the morning to my mother and twice or thrice yearly trips to see my in-laws, these visits gave rhythm and ballast to the year.

And I needed grounding. Our months-overdue house renovation lagged as if the contractor had been paid not to build but to mess with our minds. The baby and I stayed a few days with my mother and then in a makeshift bedroom on our third floor to escape the construction dust. I tried nursing on demand, but the baby and I were miserable. In desperation I reverted to an old-time nursing schedule from my mom's copy of *Dr. Spock*—the first parent power move, my husband called it. And soon enough, we were ready to roll.

At my grandparents' house, we ran through our repertoire: nurse, burp, diaper, sporadic eye contact. She nursed fast and spit up regularly, as I had done with my mother. We praised her gusto and commended her natural overflow valve. Her staccato *ah-ah-ah* charged the air in the quiet pink-and-green house. What a fine baby. I swaddled her in a new blue, too-big baby zip-bag sleeper, fastened it with a diaper pin—and put her down for her final trick, milk-induced oblivion. Excellent sleeper. Nana directed me to the end of the couch where my sister had dozed, in the same relative position in which I'd been put down to nap. We propped pillows and stood staring.

"Just think, honey," Nana said, "last week you were still pregnant."

For a moment I couldn't take it in. Now a baby girl lay sleeping among us. Last week there had been no such person making grown-ups prop pillows and move furniture. Just a few days before, I had been gravid, unable to bend, swollen with fluid, moving, eating, breathing, eliminating for two. Now I was alone again, but with less illusion of control, in a shrinking, lactating body: mother-morph, supple.

I had learned long ago that death inhered in life, silent but active. As an asthmatic child, I knew that life could be squeezed out of my narrow chest as a car sped me to the hospital. Death could take you in a breath.

But I had not known with the same certainty that life itself lay imbedded in each shiny moment. I had not known the mystery of how lightning changed amino acids into cells or of spontaneous healing. I had sung Handel's *Messiah* and loved the music, but had not dared hope that in my own flesh I would see the divine. A recovered asthmatic, I could breathe, but not yet deeply, not into each cell. I was, I am, we are all destined to die—but just as surely to participate in this moment, in creation.

The week before, I'd been pregnant. Now someone new and beautiful lay on the couch, dreaming new dreams all her own. It gave me hope where I hadn't known I was hopeless.

The Girl I Was

Kathryn Harrison

December 9, 1984. I'm in a hospital morgue, kneeling beside the body of my grandfather. He's draped in a white sheet, and like an angel, he's barefoot, dressed for annunciation. His eyes are the palest blue.

The girl who hasn't seen them yet, the girl I was before the drawer slid out, believes she and everyone she loves will live forever. She has time on her hands—enough to window-shop and to see bad movies, to smoke another joint and defer another decision, enough to stay out late and waste time kissing the wrong people. How can one night matter when she has so many?

But I'm looking into my grandfather's eyes, and I'm not that person anymore. The violence of his eyes' emptiness, their nothingness, has shaken me so my teeth chatter. I put my head down on his silent chest.

In a minute an orderly will come to close the drawer. In an hour I'll be on the phone, long distance, to a graduate school admissions director. In a week I'll have mailed my application.

In a year I'll be at school, friends with a girl like the one I was. Lighten up, she'll say, slow down, relax. You act like someone who's been given a fatal diagnosis. There's no such thing as wasting a kiss, she'll insist, and I'll try—really I will—but it won't do any good. I won't remember how to feel that way.

Questions?

Jennifer Krause

"I'm stalled," the young woman said, sitting mannequin-still in the bustle of the café where we met. Although she was grateful for a wonderful husband, beautiful children, and the valuable work she did each day, something was making her engine falter, and nothing could give it a jump. She called it a crisis of faith. Yet for her, as with many people I encounter in my work as a rabbi, it did not involve God or religion. It had to do with a broken trust in the meaning of her life—a struggle that transcends church, mosque, yarmulkes, and yoga mats; age, geography, and tax bracket. It's a trust that can break not only when you end up in a place you hoped you'd never be but also when you have everything you ever dreamed of.

"What's the point?" she asked.

"I know you want an answer," I said, "but what you need is a new question."

When you get stranded, the way to start moving again is not to search for an answer but to find a new question to which your life can be the answer. Whether you're celebrating the birth of your firstborn or marveling at her graduating in cap and gown; whether you've landed a dream job or hit retirement, are getting married or mourning the loss of a longtime love—every one of these moments is a starting point. Feeling stuck doesn't mean the meaning has gone from your life. You've just outlived one question and need to find the next—and the possibilities are endless.

True, it takes some searching to find your new question, but everyone has what I call an SPS—a Spiritual Positioning System—to guide them. This SPS is the instinct that makes you stop multitasking and lean in closer to hear what someone's saying because a sentence suddenly gives you the chills. It's the headline that stays in your mind long after you read it, prompting you to think, *Do I have a talent or an idea that could turn this problem into yesterday's news?* It's the photo of you as a girl, writing a story on your grandfather's typewriter that turns up in a drawer and makes you consider, *Is there someone I forgot I wanted to be?* As long as you keep letting life ask you another question—and reveal that there is always more for you to be and do—you are unstoppable.

The stalled woman who came to me for "the answer" didn't receive one that day, but she did get the jump start she needed with a new question. While we sipped our coffee, her SPS engaged as the conversation turned to an organization she had created. I was marveling at how she'd grown it from a staff of one to an entire devoted team. The organization had become what she'd worked for so tirelessly, but it no longer needed her in the same way—and although she certainly hadn't stopped caring about it, she suddenly realized that the passion that had driven her was gone. "I've been trying to find what's missing, figure out what I need," she said. "But the question is, what else really needs me now?"

It was only a beginning, but just sensing that there was a new answer for her to live out was the start of finding her faith—and her fuel—again.

The Pivotal Moment

Michael Cunningham

When I was a child in the early sixties, we performed H-bomb drills at school. The teacher would announce that the enemy had aimed a hypothetical nuclear bomb at our town, and we'd all crouch under our desks. In the event of an actual attack we would, presumably, wait until it was over and then, having been saved by our desks, march out into the devastation and begin our new, post-nuclear lives.

According to the Big Nuke theory, my life was to be galvanized by a singular dramatic event, after which I would be altered almost beyond recognition. As an adolescent, I tended to believe that the big event would involve having sex. Once that had been accomplished, I would no longer feel vague and uncertain, plodding, squeamish in my own skin. I would no longer feel like an idea for a person; I would begin feeling like an actual person.

I eventually managed to have sex, but found myself still alarmingly recognizable afterward. So I put my faith in love. I began waiting for romance—true, deep, and profound—to do the job.

Romance arrived (not as good as I'd hoped, but still), and it was in fact true, deep, and profound. I was undeniably transformed, but not to the degree I'd expected. I was essentially myself, in love.

I then turned my attention to success. If I could cease working in obscurity, if my stories were published to acclaim (preferably widespread), then . . . I won't belabor the point. It began to seem that transformation was going to be as much a no-show as those Soviet bombs we once believed were headed straight for our school.

And yet. At the risk of sounding inspirational, I realize that I have in fact been transformed—by sex, by love, by my work, and by uncountable other events, many of which have been less than dramatic. I was transformed at my monthly poker game, when I looked around the table and realized that I could not possibly wish for a funnier, smarter, more idiosyncratic group of people, and that my life had been good by definition, if only because it had brought me there. I was transformed sitting in the Jardin du Luxembourg on a warm September afternoon, among a throng of Parisian families and young lovers, when I imagined that if an extraterrestrial appeared before me and demanded to know why the earth should not be vaporized, I would bring him there and say, simply, "Look, we can be like this." I was transformed by my mother's death, and by winning the Pulitzer Prize, and by finding a hundred-year-old pottery shard in the water off Provincetown, still bearing a tiny blue pagoda and three birds in flight.

It's all ordinary, even that which seems enormous. It's all enormous, even that which seems incidental. We are here, it seems, to be transformed, and transformed again, and again, and again. I suspect that it never ends.

The Search

I can tell you that what you're looking for
is already inside you.

—ANNE LAMOTT

Where Do I *Find* My Me-Ness?

Alain de Botton

One of the first questions we face when we meet new acquaintances is "What do you do?" And according to how we answer, they will either be delighted to see us or look with embarrassment at their watches and shuffle away. The fact is, we live in a culture where we are defined almost entirely by our work.

This can be hugely liberating for people who are happily employed. But the problem for many of us is that we don't know what job we're supposed to do and, as a result, are still waiting to learn who we should *be*. The idea that we have missed out on our true calling—that somehow we ought to have intuited what we should be doing with our lives long before we finished our degrees, started families, and advanced through the ranks—torments us. This notion, however, can be an illusion. The term *calling* came into circulation in a Christian context during the medieval period to describe the abrupt imperative people might encounter to devote themselves to Jesus's teachings. Now a secularized version has survived, which is prone to give us an expectation that the meaning of our lives might at some point be revealed in a ready-made and decisive form, rendering us permanently immune to confusion, envy, and regret.

I prefer to borrow from psychologist Abraham Maslow, who said it isn't normal to know what we want. It is a rare and difficult psychological achievement.

To begin to find a more fulfilling vocation, it is not enough to simply ask yourself what you might like to do. Concerns about money and status long ago extinguished most people's ability to think authentically about their options. Instead, people searching for their aptitudes should act like treasure hunters passing over their lives with metal detectors, listening for beeps of joy. A woman might get her first intimation that her real interest lies in poetry not by hearing a holy voice as she pages through a book of verse but from the thrill she feels as she stands in a parking lot on the edge of town overlooking a misty valley. Or a politician, long before she belongs to any party or has any profound understanding of statecraft, might register a telling signal when successfully healing a rift between two members of her family.

We should also remember that the first ingredient usually missing when people can't choose a life direction is confidence. Whatever cerebral understanding we apply to our lives, we retain a few humblingly simple needs, among them a steady hunger for support and love. It's therefore helpful to identify—and engage with—the internal voices that emphasize our chances of failure. Many such voices can be traced back to a critical instructor or unhelpful parent: a math teacher who berated us for poor algebra skills or a father who insisted that our sister was good at art and we should stick to the schoolbooks. The forming of an individual in the early years is as sensitive and important a task as the correct casting of a skyscraper's foundation, and the slightest abuse introduced at this primary stage can unbalance us until our dying days.

A useful thought to bear in mind for anyone still struggling with a less-than-meaningful job: Work may not be where your calling resides. Indeed, for thousands of years, work was viewed as an unavoidable drudge; anything more aspiring had to happen in one's spare time, once the money had been hauled in. Aristotle was only the first of many philosophers to state that no one could both be obliged to earn a living and remain free. The idea that a job could be pleasurable had to wait until the eighteenth century, the age of the great bourgeois philosophers, men like Jean-Jacques Rousseau and Benjamin Franklin, who for the first time argued that one's working life could be at the center of happiness. Curiously, at the same time, similar ideas about romance took shape. In the premodern age, it had widely been assumed that marriage was something one did for purely commercial reasons, to hand down the family farm and raise children; love was what you did with your mistress, on the side. The new philosophers now argued that one might actually aim to marry the person one was in love with.

We are the heirs of these two very ambitious beliefs: that you can be in love and married—and in a job and having a good time. As a result, we harbor high expectations for two areas of life that may provide support but not the deep purpose we ultimately long for. To remember such history while contemplating "Who am I?" can be enormously freeing.

And although that question is one of life's toughest,

we should allow ourselves to relish it as we think about our aptitudes, and to open ourselves to all the many sources that we can derive meaning and mission from—whether it's writing poetry, leading a neighborhood cleanup, raising children, or daring the fates while flying down an icy slope on a pair of skis. We should also consider that, in the end, the answer to "Who are you meant to be?" is perhaps this: the person who keeps posing the question.

Crystal Clear

Helena Andrews

Wrapped in orange tissue paper, boxed like an engagement ring but nestled in a white Poly-Fil cloud like cheap costume jewelry, was my "power crystal." It had been sent from Southern California by Jaycee, my new healer. I'd heard about Jaycee through friends who'd gone to law school with her at Harvard. Yes, Harvard. Jaycee is a human rights lawyer by day and an energy healer by night (she's worked with some of the Kardashians and reportedly various hip-hop luminaries). Though I was raised by a hippie who harnessed healing white light for headaches, I've always been partial to Advil. However, after hearing several girlfriends gush about the "guru" who helped them through breakups and career changes, I decided to call Jaycee myself.

My problem was hard to pin down. At thirty-two, I'd

published a book and sold a screenplay. In my personal life, I had a possible leading man. But instead of feeling powerful and in control, I felt paralyzed, uncertain. When offered a full-time job, I waffled, unable to let go of some idea of myself as a professional free spirit. I even held back in my relationship, fearful of committing to a stable future. It was as if I had all the puzzle pieces but couldn't arrange them into anything meaningful. Maybe Jaycee could activate whatever cosmic guck I had stored up and help me find my intuition.

Since I'm in Washington, D.C., Jaycee and I scheduled a "distance healing session." But first, I detailed my malaise in an embarrassingly long e-mail. When I spoke to Jaycee by phone, she told me I needed clarity and that she would send me a jolt of positive energy overnight while I slept. She explained that she likes to visualize her clients, often using a stuffed animal as a stand-in. Yikes. Getting zapped with good vibrations was ridiculous enough. Now teddy bears were involved?

The next morning Jaycee e-mailed to say she'd sensed a low-grade depression in my crown chakra—the reservoir of energy at the top of my head—and that I would start feeling "shifts" over the next three weeks. I started looking for a magical alakazam, after which I'd feel better and more decisive. I found none. But the looking itself was useful. It made me realize I was craving a sign that I should take the job I'd been offered, which I already knew was a great career move. I thought a lot about something Jaycee had written to me: "You have a pretty good track record of choosing the right way, no? How often has a choice you made turned out to be disastrous?" *What am I so afraid of?* I wondered. *Proving I'm not as good, or as lovable, as other people seem to think?* The swirling snow globe I'd been living in slowly began to settle once I realized I'd been the one doing the shaking.

And then, several weeks later, my crystal arrived, like any other impulse purchase I'd ever ordered and then forgotten about. "Programmed" by Jaycee, it was meant to be worn on my body to maintain the positive energy she had sent me (and protect me from absorbing the negative energy of others). Did I need it? I considered this as I washed the crystal, an amethyst, under tap water, per the instructions. I felt a tingling at the top of my head. It could have been my crown chakra opening up, or that I hadn't had anything to eat all day. Either way, I was listening to myself. Now I think of the amethyst—which I conceal in my purse, lest I go full-on hippie—as a rabbit's foot. A reminder that I make my own magic.

The Best of Her Abilities

Paige Williams

The proctor offers me pins and pens and pegs and chips, and I sit like a lab monkey at his big oak desk, discovering the shape of my mind. My immediate assignment involves using tweezers to insert tiny steel pins one by one into equally tiny vertical slots in a heavy resin slab. "Go row by row until you've done the whole board," Tim Fitzgerald tells me. Tim is the Boston director of the Johnson O'Connor Research Foundation, an aptitude-testing organization with labs in eleven U.S. cities, and for nine hours over the next three days he'll pretty much own my gray matter.

"Am I going for speed?" I ask.

"You are indeed," he says. "So if you drop a pin, don't chase it around the room. Just leave an empty hole."

"No pin left behind," I say in protest.

"And if a pin doesn't drop all the way down, that's good enough," he says, politely ignoring me. "Don't waste time knocking it in. Just keep going, no matter how much that may disturb your sense of propriety." Already he can tell I'm a perfectionist, but for the remaining three minutes and twenty-seven seconds of this test I try not to care what he thinks—I'm too busy tweezing and slotting, tweezing and slotting. Holing the pins is like racking test tubes, only in miniature, and with the debilitating creep of hand cramp. The exercise is tedious and repetitive, but I'm digging the rhythmic monotony.

Then I fumble a pin and it lies there mockingly until the grid is complete.

"Can I put that one in now?" I ask.

Tim nods.

"It was number thirty-seven," I say.

"You counted that it was number thirty-seven? Interesting," he says, making a note, no doubt "major control issues." Which is fine. That's what we're here for: to analyze my innate strengths and weaknesses, the talents and predilections that came bundled with my DNA along with pale skin, green eyes, and double X chromosomes. Some of the answers I already know: I am unmistakably right-handed, and I'm drawn to words and art. But what else? Am I musical? Can I easily imagine objects multidimensionally? Am I unusually observant? Do I have a ready mind for foreign languages? Can I feel happy and fulfilled in a noncollaborative workplace? Can I feel happy and fulfilled in any workplace? Am I an ideas person? A numbers whisperer? What, exactly, am I inherently good at—and am I putting those innate skills to the best possible use in my career?

"What we've noticed is that when people are unhappy with their work, the most common reason is that they're not using an aptitude they possess," Tim says. "Sometimes they sense they're in the wrong field—something's missing, something's not satisfying them. Mostly it's that they think they could be doing more."

The center's typical client is a midcareer professional or a high school or college student. Most professionals get tested for one of two reasons. One, they're in the right field but possibly the wrong place within it, and they want to know what kind of environment would lead to their best work. Or two, they wake up one day and think, *Hey, wait a minute, I don't actually want to be a lawyer/chemist/ teacher.* "These people often made their career decision too soon," Tim says. "They're having a midlife crisis and reevaluating their purpose on Earth."

Testing can nudge people to rethink their careers, even start anew. Tim and the other proctors have seen this happen: the marketing executive who became a private investigator, the payroll guru who found happiness as a consultant. I'm almost positive I won't discover that I should have been a fashion designer or a brain surgeon (world, you are welcome). On the contrary, I suspect I'm in the right field (writing) but wasting my time in office-centric situations. I'm hoping for some guidance on whether I should do what I've wanted to do for months now: leave my magazine editing job to go back to teaching and writing full-time. Will the tests pick up on that? Frankly, the tests seem to pick up on everything.

The one I just took, for instance—Tweezer Dexterity— measures the ability to use small tools or do delicate tasks. "Think of a dentist or surgeon," Tim says. "You were in the ninetieth percentile, meaning you were faster than ninety percent of the population. So what this tells us is, you're fast and accurate with tiny tools."

"'Fast and accurate with tiny tools'—I like that," I say. "Could be a book title."

"And what would that book be about?"

"Bad boyfriends?"

Oh, if only there were a test for that.

The Johnson O'Connor Research Foundation's Boston office occupies an entire nineteenth-century Back Bay brownstone, four gorgeous stories of carpeted, mahogany silence. The plaque out front reads: HUMAN ENGINEERING LABORATORY. The testing program has been around since 1922; it was started by a Harvard grad and now counts among its clients large companies and colleges such as MIT, which cites the nonprofit as an employee enrichment resource. For $675 ($750 in New York), anyone fourteen and older can be tested: two three-and-a-half-hour sessions over the course of two days, plus a third session breaking down the results.

On this late-July day, my testing begins in a second-floor room that contains little more than Tim's desk, some chairs, and a few potted plants climbing toward the bright light of a bay window. Tim is a tall, good-natured fifty-one-year-old who has worked for the foundation for twenty-three years. He wears suits to the office. During testing, he wields a stopwatch, and as he leads me through exercises involving words and images and one pretend game of Ping-Pong, he makes notations on clipboarded score sheets.

I'll ultimately take twenty-eight tests. For every phase, I'm excited but nervous. I love tests but loathe errors—I obsess over some mistakes longer than many people stay married. But I'll learn that there are no mistakes here, only signposts. "People assume they're being judged, but they're not," Tim says. "There's this idea that you have to score high on everything—you don't. Really what we hope people get out of this is greater self-understanding—that this is the kind of person you are, and how to apply that to career issues."

He opens a binder to a page full of black-and-white clip art. I'm not allowed to tell you what's on the page, but let's just call it a ladder, a padlock, a cheeseburger, a schooner, a unicorn, a boot, and a pile of coins. Each time Tim flips a page, something is different, and my job is to identify the change—maybe the ladder grew a rung, or the schooner moved, or the unicorn lost its horn. The quicker you respond correctly, the better you do. My test sounds something like this:

"The padlock rotated."

"No."

"The cheeseburger has a bite out of it."

"Right."

"The unicorn's left eye is missing."

"That happened a couple of pages ago."

"Do I get penalized for a wrong answer?"

"No, you don't."

"So can I be a CIA agent or not?"

"We don't know yet."

The foundation calls this test Observation; it measures a person's memory for visual detail or subtle changes in a scene, the kind of skill that might be useful in detective work or art restoration. "We consider a significantly high score on any of these tests to be at the seventieth percentile or higher," Tim tells me. "Your score was at the ninetieth percentile."

"See, I'm thinking why didn't I score in the ninety-fifth?" I say. "Never. Good. Enough."

But Tim says this score, like every other, is significant only in terms of the overall test pattern—high and low scores mean something only once you put them all together. To me, though, there's no mystery about which way some of these will go. The wiggly blocks, for instance—the test that Tim says "brings people to their knees": Just looking at it gives me high blood pressure. Think of a big black block carved into the shape of a rolling wave, and now imagine it as four different blocks, each made up of anywhere from four to twelve topsy-turvy pieces. If you were watching video footage of me trying to reassemble the horrific wiggles, you'd see me clink and clunk my way through all the stages of test distress: optimism (happily trying to match sections), suspicion ("Are you sure these go together?"), frustration (louder clinks, angrier clunks), and resignation ("Oh, just [unladylike curse] show me").

I score in the fifth percentile, which means you will not find me designing or building bridges in this lifetime. The wiggly blocks, along with a test involving a hole punch, backgammon pieces, and Post-it notes, assure me of something I already suspected—that I have zero future in 3-D. And I'm okay with that.

I expect the math challenges to be just as much fun— i.e., not fun at all. They turn out to be kind of interesting, though. One test involves decoding a string of numbers (my score: fifty-fifth percentile, or average). In another I move numbered chips around a board to create simple calculations—and stun my math-averse self by scoring in the ninetieth percentile. But my clerical speed? "I suspect I wouldn't be crushing any hopes and dreams if I suggested you not become an accountant," Tim says.

It quickly becomes clear that I prefer tests involving visuals, sound, and words. In a test for Ideaphoria, I'm asked to handwrite an essay as quickly as possible on a given topic. "We're after the rate of flow of people's ideas," Tim explains, "and how rapidly new ideas come to mind." (Wonderful.) In Pitch Discrimination, I put on headphones and listen to pairs of tones and decide which tone is higher or lower. (Ditto.) The Tonal and Rhythm Memory tests ask me to listen to a string of increasingly complicated tones and, after the replay, circle a number corresponding to the tone that changed. Nothing about these challenges stresses me out—they feel manageable and familiar.

The other memory tests, not so much. In Number Memory, a computer screen flashes one six-digit number after another, then I'm asked to turn over my test paper and—nightmare alert—write as many of the six-digit strings as I can remember. In Silograms, I'm flashed one pair of words after another (an English word alongside a nonsense word) and later asked to remember which English word corresponds with which nonsensical partner. These are so stressful, I'm sure I've botched them both, but on Number Memory I score in the eighty-fifth percentile, and on Silograms in the ninety-fifth. If nothing else, the testing tells me that we're not always the best gauges of our own abilities.

I like the variety of the testing, the mental muscles I'm

forced to flex. When a computer screen shows me a series of line drawings, I'm to list, as quickly as possible, whatever words come to mind. *Scissors, barbell, mustache, bird . . .* In the verbal equivalent of the Rorschach test, Tim says a word and I answer with the first word I think of—he might say *peanut* and I might say *baby*, whereas the next test subject might say *butter* or *crop*. The type of answer a subject gives puts her into one of two O'Connor-devised personality groups: objective or subjective. Objectives are generalists who prefer to know a little about a lot, according to the foundation's methodology; subjectives tend to be specialists or experts. Since I've spent my entire career as a general-assignment writer, I suspect that (like most test subjects) I'd be labeled an objective, but I actually score as a subjective; in O'Connor's world, this means I prefer individualistic work. A subsequent "grip test," which measures hand strength, will, as Tim puts it, suggest something about whether I'm okay with idleness. The stronger the subject's grip, the more stifled and frustrated she may feel in a job that forces her to sit at a desk all day. No surprise here: Give me freedom.

By the third day, I'm dying to know where all this information is leading. Judging from the dossier of results—

graphs, summaries, booklets—Tim has me quantified in entirely new, or new to me, ways. And despite my deep-seated skepticism about labeling and jargon and what the cynic in me would call psychobabble, I'm hoping the analysis will reveal something fresh and marvelous, insights that might actually empower me to change my life. Everything Tim has said these past two days has made a certain sense. Besides, there's nothing wrong with listening.

We get quickly to the most important finding: I'm a combination of something called high Ideaphoria and high Foresight. Which makes me think of a high forehead. I squelch the urge to laugh, and concentrate instead on Tim's explanation. Ideaphoria was measured by the superfast handwritten test requiring me to riff on an essay answer; I scored in the ninety-ninth percentile, the "extreme end of the spectrum," he says. "For people like you, the mind's always going, one idea after another. You can't really shut that off—ever." Low scorers tend to prefer sticking to one task without interruption. "With a high score, the first thing we want to do is find a place where you can really use that flow of ideas, rather than having to suppress it all the time."

Foresight was the test where I looked at the line drawings

and wrote what came to mind. It was also high. "People like you see a lot of possibilities in almost anything," Tim says. All of this rings true, and sounds great, but, as Tim explains, it's a bit trickier than it might seem. For starters, high-Foresight people must always have a long-range goal in order to feel fulfilled, and their daily work needs to support that goal. (For me, my day job would need to feed my long-range plan to write books and teach full-time.) Complicating matters, high-Ideaphoria people generate loads of ideas but have trouble choosing just one. This, paired with the perfectionism of high Foresight, can lead to misery, because a flow of ideas means nothing if, as Tim says, "the work has to be perfect for all time."

"So, not an ideal combination," I say.

"I don't like to make that kind of judgment," Tim says. "People who are high Ideaphoria and high Foresight are the ones who end up doing the really cool things. They often have a lot of anxiety initially, but once they get going, they're determined, and they do it."

"The key phrase being 'once they get going.'"

"They're thinking not only about what they'll be doing when they're sixty," he says, "but also what will be on their tombstone—their purpose on Earth." One of the worst things that can happen to someone like me is actually achieving a goal, he says. "Because then there's an emptiness."

And it's at this point that my brain does something uncharacteristically supportive and awesome. It forms the following thought: *But if I'm always generating new ideas, wouldn't those fill the emptiness?* Reader, you have to believe me when I tell you this was a breakthrough. I've spent most of my life focused on what I'm not, but this little jargon-enabled epiphany made me realize the upside in choosing to work with what I am.

Tim helped by summing it all up: "You're a specialized communicator. You're creative and have lots of ideas. So you get passionate about something, you tell people about it, you write about it, you draw things, whatever. You're organized, and there's some musical and language aptitude going on." At my request, he also did a bit of career counseling: I should think about avoiding corporate and office work, and I should probably introduce my idea stream (torrent, really) to a little loving discipline. I should consider being a college professor, a consultant, a novelist—or a journalist. As it happens, I told him, I'm working in every one of these areas.

"Do you find that most of the adults who come for testing are in the field they're naturally suited for?" I asked.

"Most, but certainly not all."

"And people can make changes at any point in their lives and be happy?"

"Absolutely." I hope he's right. Although if he's not, there's always the tiny tools.

The Case for Thinking Big

Mallika Chopra

Ask yourself if you're thinking big *enough*. Are you setting a goal or an intention? Intentions come from the soul—they represent who we aspire to be. If you want to write a book, that's a goal, but it comes from a deeper intention: to express yourself. Setting an intention is not about imagining a BMW and waiting for it to appear; you're planting a seed in your consciousness and giving it time to bloom, maybe in a way you've never imagined. The things most people *really* want are love, connection, and purpose. Our most profound desires are pretty universal.

The Case for Starting Small

Mark Epstein, M.D.

A friend had an Indian guru who was the embodiment of love, and the guru died. Bereft, my friend went back to India and stayed with the guru's principal disciple, and one day the disciple said, "Do you want to see the precious thing the guru left for me?" Then he pulled out something wrapped in an old Indian cloth and ceremoniously uncovered a beaten-up pot. He said, "Do you see?" My friend answered, "No. What are you trying to tell me?" And with a mad glint in his eye, the disciple said, "You don't have to shine!"

I have found that idea so helpful: *You don't have to shine*. In my life, I've been lucky enough to befriend many spiritual teachers, and to see that they didn't shine, either.

They were normal people with normal problems. Of course you should try to make the biggest life possible, but be realistic. If everyone were perfect, we wouldn't be in the human realm. And we wouldn't be developing our hearts.

My Best Self

Natalie Baszile

It's February 1995. I'm twenty-eight, seven months pregnant with my first child, the guest of honor at the baby shower my friends have thrown for me. I'm decked out in a hat made of paper plates and bows, surrounded by tables strewn with pink and blue confetti and miniature plastic babies. My mother is here, sitting in a circle with the rest of us. I'm opening gifts. Mom waves her hand, gesturing. "Mine next." She sets a box the size of a sheet cake on my lap. I'm suspicious. My mother is at best an unpredictable gift giver, notorious for buying presents and then misplacing them, or for forgetting birthdays entirely. But I tear the lid off hopefully, peel back layers of tissue paper, and instantly recognize what's inside. My mother has given me my own baby book—an album covered in navy blue felt and trimmed in white rickrack—the one she started twenty-eight years ago, when she was just about the age I am now.

Each of the neatly arranged photos on the first pages is framed on a square of colored construction paper. There's ten-day-old me, no heavier than a bag of sugar, staring blankly into the near distance. There I am as a toddler, being held tenderly in my mother's arms; and at two with my dad, feeding goats at the Los Angeles Zoo—he was slim and dapper back then, with his "quo vadis" haircut and horn-rimmed glasses. A few pages in, artwork replaces the fading photos: a print of my tiny hand, my palm painted brown, each of my splayed fingers painted green, red, orange, or yellow to resemble turkey feathers. I inspect my preschool self-portrait, my first-grade report card. On the bottom of each page, in her neat teacher handwriting, my mother had written a brief narrative, a summary of my life so far: "Spokane, Washington, July 1968. Canada and Idaho. Natalie, 2 yrs, 1 month. Saw snow for the first time. Loves Cream of Wheat cereal, corn on the cob, pickles, and listening to *Snow White* on her record player. Is terrified of snails and balloons. Cries every time her bare feet touch grass."

I keep turning pages, pausing to examine the artifacts that have come loose where the glue no longer holds them in place, until I come to a piece of folded paper tucked into the crease. I open it and read what my mother had written. I look up and across the room at her as a lump swells like a sponge in my throat. "I'll be damned," I say. "I'll be damned."

I'd dreamed of becoming a journalist—a war correspondent like Sam Waterston's character in the movie *The Killing Fields*. But one day I had a conversation with my dad that caused me to shift focus. "What should I be when I'm older?" I asked him one Sunday after church. We'd driven down to Huntington Beach and were walking slowly together along the pier. "With your looks and personality, you should go into sales," he advised. "You should come to work for me." I didn't need much persuading. His approval meant everything to me, and the certainty in his tone made me think he had to be right. I guessed I'd be going into the family business.

I graduated from high school and went on to the University of California, Berkeley, starting out as a business major and then switching to economics. As hard as I tried, I couldn't make myself care about "guns and butter" or Adam Smith's "invisible hand." Each semester of those first two years, though, I treated myself to an English class as a reward for my suffering, and those hours were my happiest. I loved the English majors, how frumpy they all looked in their clogs and wrinkled khakis as they camped out in the hallways to discuss novels between classes. I spent long weekend days in the Bancroft Library reading Gloria Naylor's *The Women of Brewster Place*, Alice Walker's *In Search of Our Mothers' Gardens*, and Toni Morrison's *Sula*, breathing in the words of my literary foremothers and feeling the first stirrings of a desire to write stories of my own. I enrolled in a creative writing workshop, where each week students shared intimate tales of their struggles to figure out who they were. I'd found my tribe. I switched majors. At the end of the semester, our professor pulled me aside and whispered, "Keep writing."

On the day before graduation, I drove over the Bay Bridge to San Francisco one final time. The water glistened to my right, and the Golden Gate rose above the curtain of fog in the distance. I felt a twist of regret in my gut. I was my best self when I wrote—curious and creative, vulnerable and fearless. I couldn't imagine closing off that part of me. And yet. I'd made a commitment. I'd promised my dad that I'd come back to Los Angeles and join the family business.

He'd started out as a ketchup salesman for Hunt-Wesson Foods, then joined Kaiser Aluminum before starting his own business, Baszile Metals Service, in 1975, distributing aluminum sheet, plate, rod, and bar to the aerospace, defense, and aircraft industries.

My dad hired me as a sales associate. For the next seven years we worked side by side. Our offices were southeast of downtown L.A., near the sad trickle of the Los Angeles River and the crosshatch of rail yards, just down the street from the Farmer John slaughterhouse. On my way to work each morning, I passed trucks pulling long, reeking trailers packed with pigs, their snouts poking through the metal rails, their mud-smeared hindquarters pressing against the mesh. On hot days, the air was the color of sweet tea from all the smog and smelled like blood and death.

If asked, I could rattle off the tensile strength of 7075 versus 2024 or 6061. I knew all about B-1 bombers and which type of aluminum NASA used on the space shuttle. I told myself it was a good gig. I had job security and saw my parents every day, which most of the time I liked. But I hated aluminum. I didn't even like sales. I spent my days answering phone calls from hard-nosed, raspy-voiced purchasing agents looking for the cheapest prices and fastest delivery. Our inventory wasn't computerized for my first two years on the job, so when a customer called, I scribbled his query on a preprinted worksheet, put him on hold, and rushed to the metal cabinet against the wall, where I flipped through trays of yellowing handwritten index cards to confirm that we had the material in stock. And even when we did get computers, Dad didn't trust them, insisting that when I had an inventory question, I "check the tag." That meant going out to the warehouse—fifteen thousand square feet of corrugated steel siding, oily concrete floors, and grimy louvered windows through which pigeons flew to nest in the rafters. I walked past the planer mill and the screeching saws whose blades threw off trails of orange sparks, down the cavernous rows, where aluminum plates as thick as king-size mattresses were stacked above my head.

What could be worse than checking tags? Cold calls. Which is what Dad wanted me to do when the phones weren't ringing. He dropped a phone book on my desk and told me to get busy. My heart sank as I leafed through the listings of machine shops; my stomach churned as I dialed. "This is Natalie, over at Baszile Metals," I'd say, feigning cheerfulness. "I'm calling to see if you need any quarter-inch I beams. Or how about some anodized 7075 tubing?"

I got lunch at a food truck that swung into the parking lot around eleven A.M. As it rolled through the gates, the driver punched the horn, and "La Cucaracha" blared through the speakers mounted on the truck's roof. I got in line and paid three bucks for a greasy egg sandwich and a shrink-wrapped apple pastry, which I gobbled down in the small lunchroom behind the office. Of course, what I really wanted to do was write, which I did every evening, often until midnight, in my little apartment on South Spring Street. I dreamed of writing full-time, of getting my stories published. But I was afraid of disappointing my dad. Every time we called on customers, he'd tell them how proud he was to have me on board, and they'd praise me for being a good daughter. I'd nod and agree that I was fortunate to have such a rare opportunity.

But now here I am at my baby shower, holding my baby book—proof that writing has always been a part of me, that it's what I'm supposed to do. I read aloud what my mother had written: "Los Angeles, 1971. Natalie, age 5. Loves to read. Favorite books: *Peter Rabbit*, *The Snowy Day*, *Whistle for Willie*, and *Little Bear*. Loves to write. Natalie is always making little books and writing stories." I blink and reread the line. *Loves to write . . . is always making little books and writing stories.* As I read the note again and again, something within me falls into place. I look at my mother and mouth, "Thank you."

It will take me another four years to leave my job. By then I'll have risen to vice president of sales. On the day I finally give notice, I will walk into my dad's office, announce my plans, and underscore that my decision is final.

I know that to stay any longer wouldn't be fair to either of us. One day my dad will want to retire, and he'd be counting on me to carry the torch. He has spent his life building this business. I couldn't live with myself if I were the one who let it crumble.

I stand at his desk, bracing for his reaction. For a time he is silent. Finally, he removes his glasses and pushes back his leather cap—the one he wears every day, because he says it keeps his head warm. He leans back in his big black chair and slowly exhales. For a few seconds, he just stares at me, and as I look back at him, I see how he's aged. He's fifty pounds heavier than the young man in the photo feeding the goats. Suddenly I feel sick, knowing that I'm rejecting his dream, the one he thought we shared. I also know that what he wants most of all is to protect me. *The bottom is a long way down.* He sighs heavily, but says nothing. He nods and waves me out the door.

Outside, the sky looks brown. I get in my car and drive

over the railroad tracks, past the same sad trickle of the Los Angeles River, past the reeking slaughterhouse.

It will be fifteen years more before my novel is published; the final draft will be my thirteenth revision. Writing will turn out to be the most challenging thing I've ever done besides raising my children. I will experience pendulum swings of exhilaration and crushing self-doubt. But I don't know any of that yet. Bumping over the railroad tracks, all I know is that I'm on my way. I'm terrified, but I can't stop smiling.

Who Am I Meant to Be?

Anne Dranitsaris, Ph.D.

Forget your career. Forget your role as a mother or a wife. Forget how much money you make or how successful you are. If you're struggling with the question "Who am I meant to be?," this quiz can help you figure out what really defines you. Based on personality science, I have identified seven "striving styles," modes of thought and behavior that direct us to seek satisfaction in different ways. Although everybody is wired with all seven styles, most people have one that dominates. When you engage this innate style, you've got the best shot at fulfilling your potential; when you don't, you can feel stuck. After responding to the statements below, you will discover your striving style, learn what to do if it's backfiring from neglect, and find ideas to guide your life in the direction it was meant to go.

Instructions: Read each of the following statements and ask yourself how true it is. Then, using the scale provided (from "never" to "always"), select the appropriate number. If your first thought when rating a statement is *it depends*, think about how you would react on an average day. The more honest you are, the more accurate your feedback will be.

SCALE
0=NEVER
1=RARELY
2=SOMETIMES
3=OFTEN
4=ALWAYS

Style 1

1. Others describe me as nurturing, supportive, and helpful.

2. I have a tendency to lose sight of my own needs and focus on others.

⓪ ① ② ③ ④

3. I am more interested in relationships than goals.

⓪ ① ② ③ ④

4. When others don't appreciate my help and support, I tend to do even more for them.

⓪ ① ② ③ ④

TOTAL: _____

Style 2

1. I enjoy being the center of attention. It's also important that my work be recognized.

⓪ ① ② ③ ④

2. I am more interested in goals than relationships.

⓪ ① ② ③ ④

3. I am very conscious of my image and work hard to make sure it reflects my success.

⓪ ① ② ③ ④

4. I have a tendency to try to meet others' expectations.

⓪ ① ② ③ ④

TOTAL: _____

Style 3

1. I get pleasure from being creative.

⓪ ① ② ③ ④

2. Others have described me as too emotional.

⓪ ① ② ③ ④

3. I don't have time for shallow relationships; I am interested only in making authentic connections.

⓪ ① ② ③ ④

4. I don't feel it is important to adapt to societal expectations.

⓪ ① ② ③ ④

TOTAL: _____

Style 4

1. When presented with a new experience, I embrace it enthusiastically.

⓪ ① ② ③ ④

2. Because my interests are so wide-ranging, I often burn the candle at both ends.

⓪ ① ② ③ ④

3. I have a strong need for adventure, excitement, and novelty.

⓪ ① ② ③ ④

4. People sometimes mistake my exuberance for impulsiveness or lack of discipline.

⓪ ① ② ③ ④

TOTAL: _____

Style 5

1. Others depend on me for my insight and wisdom.

⓪ ① ② ③ ④

2. I'm driven to be knowledgeable and competent, and to understand how things work.

⓪ ① ② ③ ④

3. Under stress, I tend to withdraw and isolate myself.

⓪ ① ② ③ ④

4. I enjoy the kind of work where I can be on my own to learn or invent.

⓪ ① ② ③ ④

TOTAL: _____

Style 6

1. Others would describe me as loyal, hardworking, and predictable.

⓪ ① ② ③ ④

2. A big priority in my life is safety—for me, for my friends, and for my family.

⓪ ① ② ③ ④

3. I strive to do what is expected of me and am respectful of authority.

⓪ ① ② ③ ④

4. I tend to be wary of new things, preferring to stay with the tried-and-true.

⓪ ① ② ③ ④

TOTAL: _____

Style 7

1. I like to have the authority and responsibility to make my own decisions.

⓪ ① ② ③ ④

2. Others depend on me to know what needs to be done (and often, to do it).

⓪ ① ② ③ ④

3. I seek opportunities where I can be in charge of people and outcomes.

⓪ ① ② ③ ④

4. I often find myself advising others.

⓪ ① ② ③ ④

TOTAL: _____

Scoring: Total your numbers in each Style section. Then take the highest total and go to the corresponding Striving Style below; if you have a few "highest" scores, read the matching descriptions and see which ring most true. Many people have two or three strong striving styles, and they can all be important in leading you to the person you are meant to be.

Style 1
Striving to Help

You are a nurturer: You are caring and supportive in your personal relationships as well as in your job. Unselfish and altruistic by nature, you often anticipate the needs of those around you before they are aware of them. If there is one thing that brings you satisfaction, it's tending to others.

What to watch out for: When you're doing things for people only to feel valued, you can become resentful. And if you sense that your help is not appreciated, you may end up playing the martyr. So before giving your time to everyone else, make sure to take care of yourself (physically, emotionally, spiritually). Practice waiting until someone asks for help: While you may be able to perceive what a person needs, that doesn't mean she wants you to attend to it.

Looking ahead: It's important for you to be genuinely of service in acknowledged ways. Whether you foster a child, care for an elderly aunt, rescue animals, or support a rock star's career as her personal assistant, look for opportunities where you can help other people or bigger causes. Volunteer work has your name written on it, as do many careers: nursing, teaching, customer service, healing, social work. Don't feel pressured to run the company or lead the project; you may be even more effective as someone's right hand. And you'll likely find working with other people more meaningful than flying solo.

Style 2
Striving to Be Recognized

You are an achiever: Ambitious, competitive, and hardworking—that's you. With a clear image of who you are, you work tirelessly to make sure your accomplishments are recognized. Your drive for success extends to your family, and you invest a lot of energy in helping them live up to your expectations. Thanks to your knack for diplomacy and abundant charisma, you often inspire others.

What to watch out for: You are prone to becoming a workaholic, slaving away toward success while neglecting your personal life. Because you're driven to gain approval, you can find yourself performing for others like an actor; if you become overly concerned with your image, you end up feeling superficial. To keep your ambition under control, get involved in group activities that require cooperation. Also practice listening to those around you and think about sharing the spotlight from time to time.

Looking ahead: Any career that allows you to scale the ranks and gain recognition, status, even material rewards, lights you up. Actress, entrepreneur, salesperson, politician—you get the picture. But consider balancing your professional challenges with personal ones: Run a 10K, train for a triathlon, compete in a tennis tournament, bike from one end of your state to the other, join a debate team, or enter your purebred spaniel in a dog show. Whenever you can win at something, you're happy.

Style 3
Striving to Be Creative

You are an artist: You came out of the womb with a paintbrush in your hand. Or maybe it was a flute or a castanet or a fountain pen to go with your poet's imagination. The point is, you're an original, and you know it. Even if you don't have a singular gift, you're drawn to the arts—anything creative, for that matter—and you have a unique way of looking at the world. Your need for depth and authenticity in relationships can lead to both great joy and profound sorrow, depending on whether others reciprocate. You don't care so much about adapting to group or societal expectations; your independence and sharp intuition propel you on your own path.

What to watch out for: When fear of conformity overrides your creativity, you can assume the role of "outsider" or "orphan" and end up feeling alienated. This lone-wolf stance might be a defense against feeling vulnerable. Try to be aware that blaming others for your banishment, or pushing away those who want to get close, only makes things worse. Also, dramatizing your emotions can interfere with your creativity.

Looking ahead: As long as you genuinely express yourself, you will feel like the person you were meant to be. How you do it is irrelevant. A chef or an architect can be as much of an artist as a painter or a sculptor. Many advertising and public relations executives are also highly imaginative. Beyond work, there are opportunities everywhere you look to coax out your inner artist: You can design your own jewelry line, create an innovative blog, dream up a comic strip. Relationships are another avenue for self-expression.

Style 4
Striving to Be Spontaneous

You are an adventurer: Action-oriented, curious, outgoing, and often technically gifted, you live for new experiences. You are drawn to taking risks and aren't afraid to fail. Generally restless, you tend to job-hop or choose a field that offers constant novelty. If you had to name your favorite place, it might be the center of attention—you're a born entertainer and can easily adapt to any audience. While you collect many acquaintances, you're less likely to develop deep, committed relationships.

What to watch out for: When you can't satisfy your thirst for variety and excitement, you may see yourself as trapped, which can lead to impulsive and self-destructive behavior—drinking, drugs, breaking off relationships, ditching financial responsibilities. Try to find value in some traditions; if you learn to appreciate repetitive experiences, you won't always feel the urge to bust free. And when a new opportunity thrills you, keep in mind that just because it sounds exciting doesn't mean it's good for you.

Looking ahead: Life will have meaning for you as long as you feel stimulated. That might mean chasing twisters, exploring polar ice caps, getting a degree in dance therapy, or becoming an astronaut. It might also mean reading new books, attending workshops, or letting yourself be swept up in an intoxicating romance. As a risk-lover with a lot of energy, you're a natural entrepreneur. You'll be happiest if you change jobs every so often and travel extensively. Movement is what keeps you going.

Style 5
Striving to Be Knowledgeable

You are an intellectual: As a leader, you're often ahead of your time. As an employee, you try to surpass the competence level of peers, even managers. Incisive and curious, you're driven to deeply understand how things work. But that's things, not people. Oh, your family and friends are important; it's just that you don't need to spend hours engaging with them. Social validation isn't your goal—you're secure enough in your cerebral pursuits.

What to watch out for: When you can't find a way to be the expert, you may withdraw or simply withhold information, which can make you seem smug or arrogant. If you feel yourself retreating into your own world, seek a friend's help to pull you back. Also balance your cerebral tendencies through physical activities, like jogging, hiking, or dance.

Looking ahead: You discover who you are meant to be through accumulating insight and knowledge. So follow your curiosity. Are you drawn to learning Mandarin? Joining a philosophy society? Studying and practicing Buddhist meditation? Delving into the complexities of computer programming? Writing a historical book? Pursuits that place you near the leading edge of technology, science, psychology, academia, or business are good bets. But any situation that allows you to work independently with freedom to investigate and innovate will fuel your drive.

Style 6
Striving to Be Secure

You are a stabilizer: You are the rock in a storm, the one others lean on. Loyal and committed in your relationships, you maintain a support system of like-minded people whom you look out for. (So what if you do it behind the scenes and don't get credit?) You are careful with money, cherish the familiar, and defend the traditions you care about.

What to watch out for: Rapidly changing environments (like a shaky economy) are very hard for you. As a result of such instability, you can spiral into a state where everything seems catastrophic and you're sure life will only get worse. You can also become overcontrolling, rejecting any suggestion that doesn't conform to your idea of the way things should be. To avoid being too rigid, each month try changing one habit. Experiment with clothes, drive a different way to work, initiate conversations about subjects you wouldn't normally discuss. And when the opportunity arises to do something new, avoid the impulse to immediately say no—this may be nerve-racking, but the more you practice, the less anxious you'll feel.

Looking ahead: You find meaning in pursuing safety and certainty. Focusing on family can give you great satisfaction. Also consider planting a vegetable garden, hosting class reunions, volunteering as a lifeguard, teaching at your church or temple. In the work arena, look for positions where you're responsible for others and for making sure everyone is following the rules. You work well in any environment that is stable and consistent. Careers in government, finance, the military, law enforcement, and product manufacturing are strong options for you.

Style 7
Striving to Be in Control

You are a leader: You approach everything as though you were born to be in charge. Confident, assertive, and decisive, you know what you want and you go after it. You look out for family, friends, and community—you feel you know what's best for them—and have no fear of confronting anyone who challenges your ideas. Taking the driver's seat, you also generously donate time and energy to people and neighborhood projects.

What to watch out for: When you feel threatened, or others refuse to go along with your agenda, you can become confrontational and domineering, sometimes to the point of being dictatorial. Practice letting someone else take charge on occasion. Try meditation; it can help you become more aware of your controlling impulses and ease the anxiety that may be provoking them.

Looking ahead: You discover your purpose when you take control of your environment. For you, finding a decision-making role is key. That could mean anything from producing a play to spearheading a global campaign for something you care about. In work, you're suited for leadership positions in education, government, industry, finance, religious institutions, or politics. But you can find satisfaction anytime you're given the autonomy to do things your own way.

Leap!

Whether you believe you can do a thing or not,
you are right.

—HENRY FORD

Faith, Hope, and Sasquatch

Martha Beck

I've always loved the way cartoon characters run right off cliffs, then look down for a hapless frozen moment before plummeting into the abyss. That's the worst-case scenario we all fear when we take a leap of faith. If you've taken one recently—fallen in love, say, or adopted a llama or put a deposit on a Harley-Davidson Wide Glide in ember red with pink flames—you know perfectly well what I mean. If you haven't, don't worry; life will lead you to a precipice soon enough. It always does.

My current leap of faith is really the same old story. You know, the one where you wake up every few mornings weirdly convinced that you're in the California mountains even though you've hardly ever visited California, let alone its mountains, and this odd phenomenon continues on and off for about twenty years, and then you actually find this place where part of you feels as if it's always lived, so you donate most of your possessions to Goodwill and spend all your money moving to a piece of property where you're more likely to run across a Sasquatch than another human? That one.

The tragic thing is, I'm not kidding. This property is now mine.

Fortunately, I'm a frequent flier when it comes to leaps of faith (not because I'm brave or bold but because I seem to be mentally ill), so I have some confidence in saying that my recent behavior entails more than horrific financial planning. In fact, I believe my move has the hallmarks that distinguish a true leap of faith from sheer stupidity.

Some psychologists classify every emotion as either love (attraction) or fear (aversion). It's not unusual for humans to base almost every decision on fear: fear of rejection, fear of poverty, fear of looking dumb, and so on. But after coaching thousands of people, I've seen that fear-based decisions lead to hollow victories at best, endless regret at worst. Only love-based decisions create lasting happiness. That's why the accountant—oops, make that poet—Sara Teasdale advised, "Spend all you have for loveliness, / Buy it and never count the cost." I'm with her all the way.

Loveliness—emphasis on "love"—is the only thing worth buying.

Now, discriminating between fear-based and love-based decisions can be confusing, because leaps of faith are frightening even when the choice to make them is based on love. (Just because you really want to have a baby or run your own business doesn't mean going into labor or launching a start-up isn't terrifying.) You can gain more clarity by getting into the habit of imagining the choices you'd make if you had no fear—of failing, of losing, of being alone, of disapproval. Take a minute now to practice: What clothes would you wear tomorrow if everyone were sure to approve? What music would you listen to today if nobody else were around—not even in your mind? What books, movies, or food would you enjoy if no one ever judged you?

Going to a fearless place in your imagination will show you clearly which decisions still have fire and energy, and which lose steam without anxiety as their fuel. The former are endogenous—meaning they arise from your inner essence, not from external pressures—and they're the foundation of every great leap.

Love-based choices have one more quality their fear-based counterparts lack: They're enduring. And in this way, they make us behave like heroes—at least the kind of heroes you find in epics like *The Odyssey* or *The Lord of the Rings*. Scholars have broken down the type of story known as the hero's saga into standard parts, beginning with the hero's feeling a "call to adventure." The next step is the "refusal of the call," wherein the hero says, "Excuse me? Do I look stupid?" and goes on with normal life. Or tries to, anyway. But the calls won't stop. The same is true for any leap worth making. The calls keep coming, tapping us on the shoulder, chirping, "Hello! Me again!" until we either give in or start drinking cough syrup straight from the bottle.

In your case, the call may be a historic role model you can't stop wanting to emulate. Or an "unattainable" purpose or profession that tugs at you like a magnet. Maybe you have weird premonitions of living in Sasquatch country (see you here soon!). If following your heart's desire seems crazy but not following it is becoming more and more difficult with every passing week or month or year, your choices come down to taking a leap of faith or living with the regret of never having tried. Wouldn't you rather jump?

My clients always expect a clear and perfect moment for a leap of faith, when the seas will part, Gandalf will arrive, and action will become inevitable. I wish. The real mechanics of a leap are so much more ordinary. All you have to do, as any long-term couple knows, is set a date. The leap from your mind to your calendar is the moment of commitment. It's that simple.

Right now, set a date for any action you can take that will move you toward your heart's desire. Then tell people about it. Those same external opinions that you must ignore when making a choice can help immensely once you've chosen. My leap of faith started the day I made an appointment with a couple of real estate agents to view properties in the California woods. I still thought I was crazy, but they didn't. The combination of my heart's desire pushing from inside and various strangers pressuring me from outside kept me in motion. This is why weddings are public: The couple could bolt from the altar, but the combination of an endogenous desire and social pressure is almost always irresistible.

You'll find that many people, especially strangers, will happily support your decision to take a leap of faith. But one more hurdle remains: the very persuasive people who will not.

The hero in a classic hero's saga initially refuses the call to adventure partly on the advice of family and friends. Few people, after all, want a beloved child, spouse, or companion to set off on a possibly dangerous quest—and the nearer and dearer they are, the more likely it is that they'll protest. It takes serious cojones to leap when the people you most trust are against it. But remember, fear makes bad decisions, whether it's your fear or someone else's. Remember, too, that protective fear isn't a manifestation of love but a sort of mutation of it. So instead of giving up on your leap when everyone around you is trying to ground you, do this:

1. Think back to a flying leap that proved to be a great decision despite your initial fears: You adopted your daughter, left the security of your old job for the opportunity of a new one, got the radically different haircut that became your signature look. Recall the frightening, liberating thrill of it all.

2. Now think back to what I call a fettered lump time, when you retreated from your heart's desire in order to calm another person's fear. Feel the dullness, the disappointment, even the resentment.

3. Switch back and forth between these two sensations until they're clear and vivid.

4. If your current naysayer's advice gives you the flying-leap feeling, listen carefully; his or her advice could make your leap cleaner.

5. If the naysayer's advice feels like the fettered lump, take a deep breath and become steady and serene (hint: You'll have to fake it). Calm your loved ones. Tell them all is well. This steadfast reassurance is all they really want.

Some cartoon characters whip out hankies, improvise parachutes, and float daintily to earth. Others crash-land and pop up only slightly woozy. The more leaps of faith you take, the more you'll find your own hankies—ways of solving problems when they appear. When you crash, you'll just keep getting better at the pop-up. You'll live through every leap except the big one at the end. And even if you never leap, you'll die anyway.

This is the thinking that has brought me here, to a little house in the big woods where I'm told a repairman was recently attacked by a cougar. Personally, I think that's just a fear-based urban myth—and that he was actually accosted by a Sasquatch. It's important to get these details right as I stand in the air, looking around at my new home, at my dream come true, at the long stretch of nothing beneath my feet.

Live Like There's No Tomorrow

Danzy Senna

That was the year I was dying of a million different diseases. Which was tragic, given that I was twenty-two, just out of college, my whole life ahead of me. I didn't have any evidence, but I could feel it, a mysterious illness growing inside of me. I searched medical books for the correct diagnosis. Lupus. AIDS. Cancer. I didn't know its name, only that it was something serious and deadly.

It wasn't just illness that obsessed me in those days. I lived in a constant state of dread. My fear was like a stray dog roving the neighborhood of my life, looking for a new source of worry. I secretly wanted to write fiction, but my state of anxiety had led me to take a job that I cared nothing about. It was the kind of job that would look good on my résumé, the kind that, boring as it was in the moment, might come in handy someday.

One day my mother, concerned, I guess, by my anxious phone calls, sent me a book in the mail. It was called *The Tibetan Book of Living and Dying*, by Sogyal Rinpoche. I began to read it on that long ride from Brooklyn into Manhattan, crushed between morning commuters.

The book asked me to imagine that I was going to die tomorrow. Not the way I had been imagining but calmly, fearlessly. It asked me: Are you living today in the spirit that you would like to be living on your last day on Earth? Instead of fearing death, the book told me to prepare for its inevitable coming. Begin the process of becoming the person you want to be when you die.

When I finished the book, I didn't reach enlightenment. But the book gave me a new, decidedly un-Western way of thinking about life and death and how the two connect. And one thing was for certain: When I imagined dying tomorrow, I didn't want to be working at my job. The résumé wouldn't do me much good after I died. So I quit my job. The next year, I went back to graduate school. I began to write fiction, my secret passion, rather than putting it off for the mythical future. I stopped thinking of my life as an anxious sprint toward some fixed finish line. It wasn't that I knew that I was not dying, but rather that I knew, paradoxically, that of course I was dying, as was everyone else on Earth, and so I had better learn how to live.

A New Foundation

Eliza Thomas

I'm not a self-starter. I never could decide anything. In college I shifted aimlessly, cutting classes, pining after unavailable men. For years I floundered in dead-end office jobs and invented excuses not to take risks. Maybe I was waiting for something—God knows what or whom—to save me from myself, but before I knew it, I was over forty and not at all grown up. I was single, childless, and depressed. Time was running out.

What to do? If only I had a family of my own, I thought, all my problems would be solved. Parenthood would give me a sense of purpose! A baby would save me! I called an adoption agency. A snap decision, very unlike me. I was desperate. I made my way through a home study, insisting that I had really thought this through, that I was ready. In no time I had a referral—a newborn boy in the mountains of Peru. I was to travel the following Sunday.

Of course I wasn't ready. "Is this a nervous breakdown?" my niece asked me as I wept uncontrollably on the phone. It probably was; I fell apart that week. The night before I was scheduled to fly to Lima, I went to the local Kmart and wandered around staring at the baby paraphernalia on the shelves, taking things down at random. My child would need everything. After an hour I abandoned my half-filled shopping cart and ran sobbing to the car. I had nothing to offer.

I called my adoption worker. She said the next people on the waiting list would be ecstatic to hear I wasn't going.

This experience forced me to examine my life—something I'd been avoiding. Whether or not I became a parent, I needed to get my act together. No one else could do it for me. Since I had no plans for the future, all I could do at first was burn bridges to the past. I quit my job as an office manager (I was a terrible office manager—I don't know how the place survived me) and gave up my cheap apartment. Then I left Cambridge, where I'd lived for decades, and moved to a cabin in Vermont I'd bought a few years back with money an aunt had left me.

It was a lucky move. The cabin sat on four acres in a

narrow valley, surrounded by wild apple trees and bordered by pine groves. The beauty of the place was inescapable and consoling. But the cabin itself was tiny. It needed reliable heat, reliable running water, a new foundation. It could barely fit a bed, much less my bookcases and piano. Pipes froze. Everything froze. Everything needed fixing.

I landed another office job, but my real work was doing renovations. A friend from Cambridge offered to help, and we became a couple with a passion for construction. We cleared out brush, raised walls, added rooms. I applied plaster, stuffed insulation, painted floors. I spent all my money on concrete and saws.

Gradually, my cabin grew larger and warmer. The additions off the back gave it an unusual shape, a domino game gone awry, but they were rock solid. I loved every odd corner of it, every uneven row of shingles I'd put on myself. I've never felt so connected, so at home. I'd realized that in rebuilding my house, I'd rebuilt my life. Finally, I had something to offer.

After two years, I called an adoption agency again. This time I was looking for a child, not salvation. This time I got on the plane.

Your Life Is a Story
You Have Lived to Tell

Laura Munson

My father was fifty when I was born. As a child, I thought that was old, but he proved me wrong. For four decades I watched him thrive in a job he loved, selling freight-car parts; travel the world; and, eventually, build sand castles with his grandchildren.

When friends lament their glory days receding in the rearview mirror, their soon-to-be empty nests, their feelings of *Now what am I supposed to do with my life?*, I tell them about my father. He sometimes said, "It's heck to get old," but even when he couldn't take the stairs two by two anymore, he still had products to patent and safaris to embark on. And tales about "the olden days." As a child, I begged for these stories. "Tell me about Sunday drives in your Model T," I'd say, "or the time at the Folies Bergère when the dancing girl pulled you up onstage!" He'd smile and say, "Not bad for a boy from Granite City, Illinois."

My dad wasn't the only senior citizen in the house. One of my grandmothers, a farm girl born in the 1800s, lived with us; the other, a flapper in the Roaring Twenties, lived nearby. My friends found them strange, these old women sitting at our Steinway spinet or baking in the kitchen, but I loved curling up next to Mimi and demanding, "Tell me about heading to Chicago to become an opera singer!" I'd volunteer to serve as egg separator while Gogo made lemon chiffon pie. "Tell me about drinking Champagne from your dancing pumps!" I'd say.

Growing up on these stories, I felt woven into a dazzling legacy. As if my family members were passing the baton—*Now it's your turn.* I, too, wanted to live a life worth recounting in rapturous vignettes.

So I danced on Greek island beaches, climbed fourteen-thousand-foot peaks in Colorado, sang in choirs in majestic cathedrals, lived on both U.S. coasts, and landed, for now, in the wilds of Montana, where I am raising my children, galloping on my quarter horse through mountain meadows, hiking in Glacier National Park, and making bonfires. It's no surprise that I also became a storyteller by trade. Stories give us permission to dive bravely into our lives, to let the pluck and perseverance of others guide our own adventures. I still have stories to tell. And I'm hungry to live many more.

In some ways, sure, it'll be heck to get old. But I hear my elders whispering, "There are mountains to climb, meadows to gallop." So I will.

Tuning In

Ellen Roth

I was forty-three years old when I got cochlear implants.
Being able to hear was very odd at first. Everything sounded
like computers, or robots, and I thought there must have
been some mistake. For a year, my audiologist made ad-
justments. It was like I was a baby. I was hearing everything,
but it made no sense. I had to learn what speech sounded
like.

The first time I heard music, I cried. All my life, people
had told me they couldn't live without music. So I went to
Tower Records, put on a pair of headphones, and listened
to the Red Hot Chili Peppers. It was pretty awesome. I just
listened over and over. Then hip-hop, electronica, jazz,
classical, rock 'n' roll, country! I spent four hours there.

I had a dog, a certified hearing dog. When someone

came to the door or called my name, he would alert me. His name was Hurray. He was a toy poodle, about ten pounds, very portable. After the implants, I heard Hurray for the first time. It turned out he had three different barks: one when I got home, when he was excited; the second when he had to go to the bathroom; the third when I was leaving—he was depressed! He didn't want me to leave!

I discovered that he snored when he slept on my lap.

Before the implants, when I walked Hurray, I would of course see people. Now I could hear them say "Good morning!" I thought, *Oh, they talk to me!* And I realized that was probably why people used to be so stone-faced with me—they must have thought I was ignoring them. Now it's so precious to be able to connect.

On the other hand, the big thing I realized is that people talk too much! All day long, they talk about nothing!

Little things surprised me, too. A person breathing hard makes a sound. In my apartment, I can hear the woman upstairs walking around. When I cook, I can hear the sauce bubbling, the toaster popping up. And I've stopped slurping soup. I have deaf friends, and I can hear the sounds they make when they eat; it's like, *Okay, guys, you're making some noise here. . . .*

Not long after getting the implants, while driving my

car, I heard this *eeeee* sound. It cost me thirty dollars to have the brake pads changed. I told the mechanic, "You know, I had to pay a lot more before." And he said, "You destroyed your rotors, that's why." I guess deaf people lose out a lot on that brake-pad warranty.

At the time I got the implants, I also went back to school. For ten years, I'd been a vocational rehabilitation administrator. I became a rabbinical student and a senior vice president at a company that produces videos using American Sign Language. Now I'm a spiritual counselor. I want to understand everything.

Give Peace a Chance

Wini Yunker

I had a most boring job. I would get all dressed up—hose, dress, white gloves—just to clerk in the circulation department of a magazine called *The Military Engineer*. I was twenty-seven years old and living in Washington, D.C. It was 1961—the year the Peace Corps got started. The moment I heard about the program, I decided it was my ticket out. I just knew I'd get in with my unbeatable Kentucky charm. The first question they asked at the recruiting center was whether I had a college degree. I said no. "Well, we can't use you" was their reply. I remember it exactly—it chilled me. I walked out, embarrassed for having hoped.

Very few women from a small town like Nicholasville went to college then. I went back to my dull job and for twenty-nine years never spoke a word of what had happened. By then I was a fifty-six-year-old college sophomore needing something to keep me going. *If I can get this degree*, I thought, *I can go into the Peace Corps!* By age sixty-four, I was ready. I called the recruiting office and, ironically, the first thing they asked was whether I had a college degree. "I've gotten my master's," I said. And yes, there were tiny roadblocks. You have to be in excellent health, so I had a bunion removed to allow me to walk long distances. And I begged the dentist to pull good teeth that needed expensive caps. I wasn't going to let my dream go down the tubes because of three problem teeth. He took one look at me, heard the fight in my voice, and said, "I'll do it."

My acceptance letter arrived soon after. I'd be teaching free-market economics to high school students in Ukraine. I left with two suitcases and stayed gone for two years straight. My first week, I'd wake up in the wee hours, stare into the pitch-black night, and say to myself, *Wini, you've done it now.* I'd think of what my brother-in-law wrote: "If you've got any sense in your brain, you will not go to Ukraine." But there I was with my embroidered pillow: BLOOM WHERE YOU'RE PLANTED. That is exactly what I decided to do. In my spare time, I crisscrossed that great country by train and made lasting friendships. I do not cower at anyone's "no" now. That Peace Corps' "no" lit my fire when I most needed it. And I see that I can live out my dreams in my own time.

Trials and Error

The best way out is always through.

—ROBERT FROST

If All Else Fails . . .

Elizabeth Gilbert

I've always considered myself lucky that I do not have many passions. There's only one pursuit that I have ever truly loved, and that pursuit is writing. This means, conveniently enough, that I never had to search for my destiny; I had only to obey it. What am I here for? No problem! I'm here to be a writer, and only a writer, from my first cigarette to my last dying day! No doubt about it!

Except that two years ago, I completely lost my life's one true passion, and all my certainties collapsed with it.

Here's what happened: After the unexpected success of *Eat, Pray, Love*, I diligently sat down to work on my next project—another memoir. I worked hard, as always, conducting years of research and interviews. And when I was finished, I had produced a first draft that was . . . awful.

I'm not being falsely modest here. Truly, the book was crap. Worse, I couldn't figure out why it was crap. Moreover, it was due at the publisher.

Demoralized, I wrote a letter to my editor, admitting that I had utterly failed. He was nice about it, considering. He said, "Don't worry. You'll figure it out." But I did worry, because for the first time in my life, I had absolutely no passion for writing. I was charred and dry. This was terrifyingly disorienting. I couldn't begin to know who I was without that old, familiar fire. I felt like a cardboard cutout of myself.

My old friend Sarah, seeing me so troubled, came to the rescue with this sage advice: "Take a break! Don't worry about following your passion for a while. Just follow your curiosity instead."

She was not suggesting that I ditch my passion forever, of course, but rather that I temporarily ease off the pressure by exploring something new, some completely unrelated creative endeavor—something that I could find interesting, but with much lower emotional stakes. When passion feels so out of reach, Sarah explained, curiosity can be a calming diversion. If passion is a tower of flame, then curiosity is a modest spark—and we can almost always summon up a modest spark of interest about *some-thing.*

So what was my modest spark? Gardening, as it turned out. Following my friend's advice, I stepped away from my writing desk and spent six months absentmindedly digging in the dirt. I had some successes (fabulous toma-toes!); I had some failures (collapsed beanpoles!). None of it really mattered, though, because gardening, after all, was just my curiosity—something to keep me modestly en-gaged through a difficult period. (At such moments, believe me, even modest engagement can feel like a victory.)

Then the miracle happened. Autumn came. I was pull-ing up the spent tomato vines when—quite suddenly, out of nowhere—I realized exactly how to fix my book. I washed my hands, returned to my desk, and within three months I'd completed the final version of *Committed*—a book that I now love.

Gardening, in other words, had turned me back into a writer.

So here's my weird bit of advice: If you've lost your life's true passion (or if you're struggling desperately to find passion in the first place), don't sweat it. Back off for a while. But don't go idle, either. Just try something different, something you don't care about so much. Why not try following mere curiosity, with its humble, roundabout magic? At the very least, it will keep you pleasantly distracted while life sorts itself out. At the very most, your curiosity may surprise you. Before you even realize what's happening, it may have led you safely all the way home.

Turn of the Tide

Amy Hempel

The triumph of intuition over reason—that is how I think of the early seventies in San Francisco. I was flunking organic chemistry, a class required in the pre-med program to get into veterinary school. The rational response would have been to hire a tutor and tough it out. Instead, I went to the beach.

I knew only one person in all of L.A., I had no job, just an overwhelming sense that I should live at the beach. I was not a surfer, not even a swimmer. But I moved into an apartment that was five steps from the boardwalk in Venice. It was already a scene, with bikers, burnouts, gangs, artists, and the early film people and galleries. My new goal? For my footprints to be the first of the day, after the lifeguards dragged rakes attached to their Jeeps across the sand.

I read tide tables on the nearby Santa Monica pier. I felt lost but calm, sitting under palm trees or swaying in the waves. I watched my crazy neighbors: Howard threw his wife's dentures on the roof during a fight, Janet worked in a travel agency whose motto was We Never Knowingly Ruin Your Vacation. The person I knew in L.A., my best friend, started to die.

Several years later, in New York City, I started to write. My first book featured the dentures, the travel agency, the Jeeps dragging rakes, my friend. Central to each story was the beach.

It's All About What You *Do*
with Your Breakthrough

Martha Beck

Try something for me: Close one eye, then spend a minute looking around. Scope out the room, admire the view, scrutinize objects near and far. Now open the closed eye.

Boom! Right?

You can see pretty well with one eye, but the stereoscopic image you get with both is richer, deeper, and more beautiful. Guess what? Life works in a remarkably similar way. You can live years, even decades, with an obstructed view of the world—believing ideas that are false to be true, holding fast to things that don't really matter—until the day your point of view is so thoroughly rattled that you finally see what's what. That experience is often referred to as a breakthrough. It's a shift in your understanding of the world, because the lens through which you view it has been suddenly, gloriously changed. And boy, do breakthroughs feel amazing. They help us live better by helping our outlook match up with reality.

Yet having breakthroughs isn't the point. Living them is. Seeing in a new way is only the beginning.

I watch people experience psychological and emotional breakthroughs fairly regularly. It's much rarer to see someone actually putting their new insights into practice. Take my client Laura, who had a huge meaning-of-life breakthrough at a weekend yoga retreat. She experienced what yogis call "the third eye opening."

"My sense of physical boundaries disappeared," she told me. "I saw that everything is a part of me, and all that matters is love."

Then Laura went home to discover that she was being audited, her dog had eaten her new leather couch, and her teenage son was smoking pot. For a second there, a whole lot of things seemed more important than love.

This is the tricky thing about breakthroughs: Many aspects of the experience may feel unpleasant, both before and after your thinking changes. As a breakthrough nears, you might feel intensely trapped, seeing no way out—which only makes sense; if you had a way out, the internal pressure wouldn't become sufficient to spur you toward change. After the breakthrough, the work required to sustain it in the face of life's audits, ruined couches, and secret dime bags can feel insurmountable.

"But you know what?" Laura told me. "Those things were hard, but they still weren't more important than what I had learned at that yoga retreat." Amen.

Laura sustained her breakthrough by deliberately focusing and building on it. She journaled and meditated about her experience. She discussed it with friends. She found books and videos that resonated with her new insights. Slowly and calmly, Laura tackled the problems that threatened to pull her back into old fear-based patterns. That's the key to sustaining a new insight: eliminating whatever threatens to recloud your vision. Hold tight to your breakthrough, because once your eyes have been opened, trust me when I say that it will not feel good to close them again.

A deliberate campaign of reminding can work for you, too. Remind and remind yourself of your new insights, until you're literally "re-minded." Your thoughts will change. Your moods will change. Your life will change.

You'll be living in a whole new world, not because you've gone to new places, but because you're looking through new eyes.

Need a little help seeing your life in a new way? Try this exercise. Be sure to finish Part 1 before moving on to Part 2.

PART 1

Fill in the blanks below as honestly as you can. Don't hold back. To start, think of the most stuck person you know. Ready? Begin.

1. This person is getting in his/her own way by being so:

   _____

2. This person could really break through if he/she would only:

   _____

3. This person is actually just afraid of:

   _____

4. If this person knew what was good for him/her, he/she would:

   _____

5. Meanwhile, I also know someone brave enough to do anything he/she wants. The quality that makes this person so amazing is:

_____

6. I'm grateful that this person didn't give in, but instead behaved in a way that was:

_____

7. If I had this person as a mentor, I'd have the guts to:

_____

8. If this person were mentoring me, what I'd love to hear him/her say is:

_____

PART 2

Have you finished Part 1? Now complete Part 2 by copying each answer from Part 1 into the corresponding blank below. Don't think as you write, and don't tweak your words. If you really want a breakthrough, faithfully copy what you wrote.

1. I can think of times when I was: (*copy your answer to question 1 in Part 1*)

_____

2. I really need to just: (*copy your answer to question 2 in Part 1*)

_____

3. I'm really just afraid of: (*copy your answer to question 3 in Part 1*)

_____

4. If I knew what was good for me, I would: (*copy your answer to question 4 in Part 1*)

_____

5. On the other hand, what makes me so amazing is: (*copy your answer to question 5 in Part 1*)

_____

6. I can recall times when I've had the courage to behave in a way that was: (*copy your answer to question 6 in Part 1*)

_____

7. Deep down, I have everything it takes to: (*copy your answer to question 7 in Part 1*)

_____

8. My true self is always guiding and comforting me. Right now it's saying: (*copy your answer to question 8 in Part 1*)

_____

Now read through Part 2. Open your mind to ways in which it might be accurate. Take your own advice. And see if your viewpoint doesn't start to expand into something greater than you ever imagined.

The Trust Muscle

Barbara Graham

—⁑—

It was the perfect day for a wedding. The sun shone brilliantly without being oppressively hot. The musicians had just played a glowing rendition of Mozart's Flute Quartet in D. Best of all, the people I loved most in the world were gathered in the storybook garden where Nick and I had begun to recite our vows. Even my closest friends—a notoriously picky bunch—had unanimously approved our match. So why wasn't I happy? Why was my pledge to love Nick "until death do us part" making me feel as though I might perish on the spot? Why did every cell in my body shriek, "I don't!" when I whispered, "I do"?

It didn't take a long time for me to realize the marriage was a mistake. I'd had a sinking feeling in my stomach ever since Nick had popped the question. But instead of paying attention to my feelings—including the absence of sizzle from our very first date—I focused on the many advantages our union would have to offer. The list contained everything I'd been conditioned to want: a nice man with a promising future, a steady income, and a good home in which to raise my son. What more could a girl possibly ask for? A lot, it turns out. A year later, Nick and I parted ways.

I've since learned that each time we ignore our inner voice, we shrink a little inside ourselves. And the more we second-guess that voice, the more we fear that if we rise up to our full height and declare our truth, we'll be rejected, reviled, abandoned, unloved. But the opposite is true.

As babies, we know instinctively what's right for us and what isn't—and we coo and cry accordingly. But eventually we start to forget. Instead of relying on what we know in our bones, we seek the approval of others, strive to make them happy, and try to live up to their expectations. We bend over backward to be "good" people, to make the "right" decisions, to be "successful," to do the ten thousand things we believe we're supposed to do. "In trying to please other people," the Greek philosopher Epictetus said, "we lose our hold on our life's purpose." And over time, our inner voice grows increasingly faint.

The good news is that self-trust is a muscle that can be

strengthened. Start by noticing the moments when you're tempted to betray your truth—from the little white lies you tell to make someone like you ("Yes, I adore bungee jumping!") to choosing inappropriate boyfriends or taking a new job for all the wrong reasons.

Of course, it's possible to be so overwhelmed by fear and confusion that you won't have a clue what your real feelings are. But your body knows, and if you pay attention to its signals—the knot in your stomach, your racing heart—you'll gradually start to pick up on your true worries and desires. Once you realize your own truth, you'll need to act on that knowledge—which is not always easy. Sometime this involves making choices that run counter to what your husband, boss, best friend, hairdresser, personal trainer, astrologer, or shrink advises. At those times, think of all the mythic stories you've heard: the bestselling novelist who kept faith with herself and continued sending out her manuscript after it had been rejected by thirty-seven publishers, the brilliant inventor who never gave up on his idea, even when his scientific peers laughed at him.

Living more authentically, without your habitual safety nets, will often stir up anxiety and discomfort. But it will also bring exhilaration and joy. Even when you make mistakes—and there will definitely be mistakes—they'll be *your* mistakes. Owning them and standing tall inside yourself despite your blunders will help strengthen your burgeoning trust muscle. As much as I wish I hadn't married a man I didn't truly love, I know that even if a fortune-teller could have predicted my marriage would fail, it was a blunder I had to make.

Each day offers a thousand opportunities for us to practice. Do you speak up when a colleague makes a remark that offends you, or do you stand quietly by, swallowing what you believe in your heart? When a friend asks you to help her move during your busiest time at work, do you say yes automatically because you're afraid if you don't she won't love you? At moments like these, remember your intention to trust yourself. Stop, take a breath, and give yourself time to assess how you truly feel. As with building—and maintaining—any muscle, repetition is the key. The more you trust yourself, the stronger and more confident you will become.

Rejected? Lucky You!

Suzanne Finnamore

I am a writer, but that's not what I aspired to be. I wanted to be a dancer. I took classes for twelve years, often crawling to the bathroom on all fours in the morning because I could not stand up, my muscles stretched way beyond their limit.

After surviving the audition for an elite dance class at the University of California, Berkeley, I felt I was on my way to realizing my dream. One semester later I was called into the dance director's office and told I didn't have what it takes. For one thing, I could not do a pirouette. For another, I had breasts and, according to tradition, those just get in a dancer's way. Marinating in defeat and shame, I watched *The Turning Point* compulsively and felt ill.

I was demoted to the general phys ed dance class. After

a few weeks, I had to admit it was more fun than the highly structured and competitive environment of the elite class. I also declared a new major: English literature. Although this was my second choice, it became clear after I joined the workforce that it was the right one for me. The job opportunities were a lot better, as were my long-term prospects for happiness. Reading and writing don't give you shin splints, and you can do them when you're ninety.

It was in a college poetry-writing class that I met my first big love, Reed. He admired my poems and looked like a young Marlon Brando. We dated until the end of the school year, when he informed me that he still loved his ex-girlfriend. I was so devastated that I skipped my own graduation—I could not bear the thought of seeing them together.

Reed became a minister, a good one from what I hear. We are still friends. And because he dumped me, I developed into an autonomous woman who surely never would have emerged had I married straight out of college. Also there is this: Would I have made a good minister's wife? Probably not. Minister's wives don't wear black boots, they don't drink, and they rarely, if ever, say "s***fire."

Eventually I learned that I can survive heartbreak, and I wrote more poems. This led to being published in

Ms. magazine, the brainchild of my idol Gloria Steinem. All told, I earned $150. I decided to try my hand at commercial copywriting, which pays somewhat more amply.

I remember preparing a massive presentation five years into my first advertising copywriter's job. It was a presentation for a gaggle of car dealers who were meeting at a fancy resort in Maui. I had worked hard to add the finishing creative touches, but just as I completed the task, my boss informed me that although most of my colleagues were bound for Hawaii, I would not be attending the meeting. That day I revised my résumé and faxed it to the creative director of a large agency in San Francisco. The timing was ideal; the agency had just landed a huge account. I was interviewed by a woman who ignored my hideous portfolio of car ads and just liked the honest way I described my job and my frustration with it. She met me on a Saturday and called with an offer the next Monday—and within an hour, I gave my two-week notice. "Don't get mad, get even" is not my motto. My motto is, "Do feel angry and don't just get even—go to a much higher place where they can't see you from their lawn chairs, which are probably missing slats."

My first novel was rejected by no fewer than nineteen

publishing houses. I shelved it. As a teacher of Anne Lamott's once told her, "Every writer has a novel that isn't published. This will be yours." I felt bruised but not broken. I retained a wild optimism based on youth and the encouraging nature of many of the rejection letters. Several editors stated that I obviously had talent. But, they gently added, I had forgotten to include one small detail: a plot. I made a mental note: Remember to have a plot.

One rejection was harrowing, though. In spidery handwriting, a somewhat famous editor said I was "intoxicated with my own style." It was like a dagger to my spleen. Yet within hours I realized he was right. I was intoxicated with my own style. I never forgot that. Had he been kinder and more tactful, I would not have gotten the point. That's how I learned that sometimes the cruelest cuts are the most needed. Rejection can be like mulch: dirty, smelly, and essential to growth.

I eventually wrote another novel, which I eagerly submitted to my agent. After three silent months, I received a thick envelope containing my manuscript and a letter in which the agent tersely explained that she felt there was no market for the book.

After a four-month depression, I decided she was wrong.

Sometimes setbacks make you feel that perhaps you have made your goal too small—you need to aim not lower but higher. What the hell, in other words.

Marshaling my courage, I sent ten query letters to agents in New York. Within days I had my replies. Not one but two agents wanted to represent me. The one I chose became my fairy godmother. She sold the book immediately, as well as the film rights. I resisted the impulse to contact my ex-agent to inform her of the good news. I decided she should have the thrill of discovery.

Don't get me wrong. I detest rejection. And I do take it personally, even though, according to self-help mavens, I am not supposed to. Yet I am too stubborn to admit defeat for long.

I think that, especially in matters of work, you should expect rejection on a regular basis. To try to avoid it is a major mistake, as you will massage your unique style into the consistency of gruel in the vain effort to try to please everyone all the time. In general, the populace will be divided into four groups: (1) people who understand and appreciate what you are trying to do, (2) people who understand and don't appreciate it, (3) people who don't understand and appreciate it anyway, and (4) people who don't understand and hate your guts. It is not important that everyone fall into the first category; it is only important that you put yourself out there.

It is also key to listen and watch for the message the rejection has hidden in its folds. At forty I now believe rejection is God's way of kicking you to higher ground. That said, I still sometimes grow tired of God's boot print on my behind.

When a county deputy served me a petition for divorce, I placed it in a desk drawer, unable to endure its typed finality. One day soon afterward, I took it out and taped it to the refrigerator door. I needed to see it, to absorb the harsh reality that my marriage was over. The next day, I found a hawk feather on my front porch. A few days later, I found another hawk feather in almost the exact same spot. It was no accident. I believed I was being alerted to the possibility that, from a distance, this vast rejection was a blessing in disguise. I placed the two feathers above the petition and felt a little less sad.

Divorce is not something desired; I think it is often a terrible mistake with far-reaching consequences. Yet I know the law of balance works, and probably I will reap manifold gifts from my brief marriage. When I look at my son's face, I see I already have.

As long as I am alive, I will be rejected. We all will. I

try to loosen up, to become more of an observer, as though I am watching a film whose plot twists and turns only enhance the eventual resolution. It's just plain interesting to go through big changes, to feel improved as a result of pratfalls, turnarounds, and upheavals. Rejection? Bring it on, I say. Bring it on.

Second Acts

I never quite believed that
one chance is all I get.

–Anne Tyler

Never Too Late

Robin Black

—✳—

Dear fellow late bloomer, I thought you could use some advice. I know I would have benefited from some along the way, but back when I most needed it, there wasn't much to be found. I earned my MFA in writing in 2005, when I was forty-three years old and, much to my distress, the phrase "young emerging artist" seemed to be everywhere. There were prizes for young emerging artists; there were words of wisdom for young emerging artists; there were lists of the most exciting young emerging artists to watch. Anxious to find my peers, I did an online search—only to be told: "Your search for middle-aged emerging artists has yielded no results."

Clearly the search engines weren't looking hard enough. Because as you and I both know, there are plenty of us out here—along with the middle-aged emerging doctors, nurses, professors, jewelry designers, yoga instructors, cupcake masters, and more: an entire civilization's worth of people who for one reason or another got off to a late start. And I'm not going to sugarcoat that for you. We are late. For me the original dream of publishing a book by age twenty-five became thirty, then forty, then forty-five—until reality stepped in with its final answer: book by fifty. Am I glad about that? Let's just say it took some readjusting.

The point is, there are challenges to changing your life radically when you've already done a bit of living. The first challenge, of course, is actually to do it—whatever it is. In the past few years, more women than I can count have told me that they too have thought of embarking on new careers, often first careers, in their thirties, forties, or fifties—even their sixties—but can't bring themselves to act on their dreams. "Nobody would take me seriously," they say. Or "I can't compete with all those young people." Or "Are you crazy? I have a mortgage."

I wish I could say that those concerns aren't real, but unfortunately they often are. I remember when I started writing, just before I turned forty, how unseriously many people took my pursuit. Time after time I would work up the nerve to say, "I've recently started writing," and time after time the response would be a patronizing "Oh, that's nice," or a little smile and a subject change.

It turns out that beginning a new career in midlife requires you to take yourself seriously enough that your confidence won't be shattered if other people don't. This is especially true if you've been a stay-at-home mother for any length of time. Sure, everyone talks a good game about full-time mothers being no less capable or interesting than women who seek careers, but tell someone you've spent the past fifteen years caring for your children, and you can almost see them docking your IQ.

Here, though, is where we late bloomers have an advantage: One of the great things about getting older is that other people's opinions have less power over us than they once did. I work with a physical therapist who recently told me, "When I turned forty, I stopped worrying about offending other people. When I turned fifty, I started enjoying offending other people." In many ways this is the best time to do something that others might view with skepticism, and to risk a little ridicule that might once have been unendurable.

As for competing with young people—well, again, it would be nice to say that it isn't an issue, that we're all on a level playing field, but in the vast majority of careers that just isn't the case. You might think publishing would be age-blind. After all, as a literary agent once reminded me, writers use their minds, not their bodies. "You aren't tennis players," she said. "You aren't models." But publishing involves selling, and youth sells; even in my field there are a surprising number of career-enhancing accolades available only to the young, like the *New Yorker*'s list of 20 Under 40 and the National Book Foundation's annual 5 Under 35 Award. I could spend hours grinding my teeth over the unfairness of that, but what would be the point? I already know life is unfair.

Financial concerns, alas, aren't so easy to brush off. Many late bloomers are shouldering entire families financially—which is why many find themselves juggling an old career alongside an emerging new one, eking out hidden minutes from already overfull days. Among my graduate school classmates were teachers, lawyers, newspaper reporters; in their "spare time," they were writers, too. Somehow the fear of never having done the thing they felt most drawn to outweighed the difficulties of doing it.

That doesn't mean it's easy to overcome every obstacle. In those of us whose professional accomplishments didn't come with youth, there is often an ancient well of insecurity—a reservoir of fear deep enough to have kept us from pursuing our dream careers in the first place. I know this firsthand. While I was still in college, my mother became the first woman dean of Columbia Law School, which at the time was front-page news. (She even got to be a clue on *Jeopardy!*—the ultimate prize of fame!) My father had a long, distinguished career as a legal academic and civil rights advocate, including having been one of the lawyers responsible for the winning brief in the landmark school desegregation case, *Brown v. Board of Education.* Throughout my youth, when I wasn't hearing from young women what an inspiration my mother must be to me, the rest of the world was looking at my father and noting what big shoes I had to fill.

I opted not even to try. There are doubtless children who would have responded to the same situation with focused, intense ambition, either to carry on the family legacy or to best it. Not me. I had a baby at twenty-five and left the world of professional accomplishment alone.

I suspect that lots of people who reach middle age with ambitions they've never even tried to fulfill have similar stories. If not parents with intimidating careers, then parents who insisted on standards they feared they couldn't meet, or parents who seemed perpetually disappointed in them, or households in which achievement was given less attention than failure. For many of us, early career decisions were equal parts running toward and running away. And if you are in that category, as I am, then as you contemplate embarking on a new career, you not only have to face down the issues we all do as the years pass, you also have to confront some powerful old inner demons. For me that was a process that included therapy over many years, but therapy isn't the only route. I have friends who meditated their way past fear.

No matter your method, it's hard to imagine that ridding yourself of paralyzing inhibitions can be anything but good. Which brings me back to my first piece of advice, the most important one: Do it. Whatever it is. If you have a dream, go ahead, take the risks, and make whatever sacrifices you possibly can. Endure the funny looks. Ignore the ridicule if ridicule comes. Expect some unfairness along the way, and kick up a fuss about it if kicking and fussing feel productive. Whatever you do, keep moving forward.

Many people have said to me, "Better late than never, huh?" and I suppose there's truth in that. But think about yourself as a very young woman, then think about who you are now. Maybe it's more a case of better late than early. Maybe, after all, it's not even that late. Think about who you want to be ten years from now. Then get to work.

What's Holding You Back?

Valorie Burton

You dream of a more fulfilling career. So why don't you go for it? For most women, the biggest obstacle is fear. Valorie Burton, founder of the Coaching and Positive Psychology Institute, created a quiz that will help you discover what you're most afraid of.

1. You read on your company's Web site that there's an opening in another department. The job has more responsibilities, and the rewards are big. You . . .

    A. Assume that the candidates from within that department will have more experience than you.

    B. Wonder how you'd tell your boss if you applied. She thinks you're happy working for her.

C. Get anxious about the stress the position would entail. What if you couldn't keep up?

D. Decide that rocking the boat at this stage in your career could be disastrous.

E. Apply. What have you got to lose?

2. The business you launched on the side starts to take off—so much so that you could quit your nine-to-five. You . . .

A. Draft a letter of resignation. If this venture doesn't work out, you can always return to your old career.

B. Picture yourself going bankrupt and ending up a penniless bag lady.

C. Fret about whether you have the skills to run a business. This bout of success could just be beginner's luck.

D. Remember all the people who doubted your business plan. They'll think you're nuts to quit your day job.

E. Balk at the idea of being solely responsible for your paycheck.

3. You always wanted to teach but were discouraged by the pay. Thanks to your spouse's recent raise, you could probably manage on a smaller income. You . . .

A. Question whether you have what it takes to command a room full of unruly seven-year-olds.

B. Worry that you really wouldn't be able to maintain your lifestyle on a smaller salary.

C. Feel the pressure already. Sure, you'll be passionate about teaching in the beginning, but don't teachers get burned out?

D. Dismiss the idea as irresponsible. What if your spouse gets fired?

E. Talk to your spouse about the financial ramifications of changing paths.

4. You work for a start-up. Your boss just got fired and you'd love to step into her role. You . . .

A. Meet with the hiring manager and make a case for yourself. If she thinks you're right for the job, she'll give it to you.

B. Fear it's too risky: If you get axed like your boss did, it would sabotage the rest of your career.

C. Decide you're not ready yet. You'd like to have a few more years of experience before you move up the ladder.

D. Deny your interest because you don't want to appear presumptuous.

E. Feel confident that you could do the job but unsure that you want the company riding on your shoulders.

5. Your doctor suggests your recent health issues are stress-related. She tells you to cut your hours and take regular vacations. You . . .
   A. Hesitate to make changes because you don't want your performance to suffer.
   B. Worry that your colleagues will resent you if you leave at six.
   C. Think, *If I seem more energetic, my boss will just give me more work!*
   D. Rule out the idea of a vacation. In your absence, your boss could realize she doesn't really need you after all.
   E. Agree with your doctor. A break might even make you more productive.

6. You were just laid off from your long-term job at a marketing firm. This could be the perfect chance to pursue your dream job as an interior designer. You . . .
   A. Feel nervous but excited: Now's the time to take a leap.

B. Dread the prospect of starting at the bottom of the ladder. You'd be throwing away all your years of marketing experience.

C. Laugh off interior design as a pipe dream. So few people survive in that industry.

D. Imagine what people might say: You're too old to compete with young, hip designers.

E. Admit that you have a good eye but cringe when you imagine the expectations of actual paying clients.

7. You've been thinking of writing a novel for years. Your best friend asks you why you don't get started now. You . . .

A. Tell her how difficult it is to find a publisher, especially for your first book.

B. Explain that you don't want your employer to think you're not fully committed to your day job.

C. Admit that you're anxious about putting yourself out there. People might see that you're not as great a writer as they thought.

D. Lay out your nightmare: You'd suffer from writer's block and waste years of your life trying to finish the manuscript.

E. Thank her for the encouragement and resolve to start writing this week.

8. You've worked in a bank for eight years, but you're tired of sitting behind a desk. You feel drawn toward nursing.

    A. Vow to give it a shot and enroll in some night courses.

    B. Make a mental list of all the reasons nursing is a bad idea. You might catch a hospital-borne infection, for example.

    C. Obsess about whether you'd succeed in nursing school. You were never such a great student, after all.

    D. Reject the idea because you'd need help paying for school, and you'd hate to ask for it.

    E. Wonder if you can handle the responsibility, day in and day out. People's lives could depend on you.

Answer Key

Tally which letters you circled the most in response to the odd-numbered questions and the even-numbered questions. Then refer to the corresponding section below for advice on how to overcome your most prominent fear.

Fear of Failure

    Odd numbers: Mostly "A" responses
    Even numbers: Mostly "C" responses

You are terrified of stepping outside your comfort zone. And you're not alone—I find that this is the most common fear. My clients who struggle with it are often perfectionists who tend to take failure personally. When they don't succeed, they say, "I'm a failure," rather than "I failed." So it's understandable that new ventures can seem frightening. The most important thing you can do for yourself is work on building self-efficacy—the belief that you can actually accomplish what you want to do. Start by setting and achieving small goals. For example, if you want to be a massage therapist, sign up for an adult education course in shiatsu. If you want to be a florist, reach out to one; invite her for coffee and ask her how she got started. As you succeed at these smaller challenges, bigger goals will seem less daunting, and eventually you will develop the confidence to take the leap you've been dreaming about.

Fear of Success

Odd numbers: Mostly "C" responses
Even numbers: Mostly "E" responses

You're fairly confident in your abilities, but you balk at the pressure of maintaining success once you have it. You know that your achievements will breed higher expectations, and you worry that you won't be able to meet them. You may even be experiencing what psychologists call impostor syndrome, the fear that those around you will discover you're not really as talented or competent as they think. People who fear success often credit their achievements to circumstances rather than to their talent and other assets. The key for these people is to accept responsibility for their accomplishments. Many of my clients find this simple exercise helpful: Think of a recent success—say, a new account that you won. Now make a list of the skills and qualities you drew on to win it—determination, intelligence, creativity, charm. . . . (If you're struggling, ask a friend for help; others can often see your assets more clearly than you can.) Make this exercise a habit each time something goes well at work. Once you begin to see your strengths in action every day, you will recognize that you are, in fact, well equipped to tackle whatever challenges lie ahead.

Fear of Disapproval

Odd numbers: Mostly "B" responses

Even numbers: Mostly "D" responses

You seek permission before you make changes, and you can get stuck when you think it won't be granted. My clients who are addicted to approval often didn't get enough of it when they were younger. As adults they tend to look to titles and salary for validation. People in this category also shy away from asking for help, to avoid rejection. This can be a crippling fear, because pursuing your dreams requires support, whether it's financial or emotional. To move forward in your life, you need to start valuing your own approval more than others'. This is, of course, easier said than done. It takes work. I tell my clients to write themselves permission slips for what they want: I give myself permission to take a vacation. Or I give myself permission to volunteer in a different field. This may sound silly—in fact, I know it does. But the exercise can be very useful because it prompts you to remember this crucial fact: You don't need anyone else's permission but your own.

Fear of Losing Control

Odd numbers: Mostly "D" responses
Even numbers: Mostly "B" responses

You feel overwhelmed by the prospect of change and worry that if you follow your heart, you will risk everything— your financial security, your future, even your relationships. When faced with a decision, "catastrophizers," as psychologists call them, tend to jump to the worst-case outcome. For example, when you think about changing jobs, you quickly come to a vision of yourself living on the street after failing miserably. Karen Reivich, Ph.D., co-director of the University of Pennsylvania's Resiliency Project, has a useful technique for easing that anxiety. When you feel your negative thoughts spiraling out of control, try forcing them in the opposite direction by imagining an equally improbable best-case scenario. For example, you are so amazing at your new job that you get promoted five times in the first year and appear on the cover of *Forbes*. This positive picture broadens your outlook and makes it easier for you to envision a realistic scenario between the two extremes. You will likely struggle a bit as you transition into the new job, but you will gradually become more successful—and feel much happier and more satisfied.

Ready for Change

Odd numbers: Mostly "E" responses

Even numbers: Mostly "A" responses

Congratulations! You understand an important truth: Everyone feels fear. And you know that the secret to success is not letting fear stop you. With practice, you've developed the courage you need to move forward despite your anxieties. Your confidence will allow you to explore other paths and stay the course when you encounter bumps on the road.

The White Room

Elizabeth Kaye

❖

There must have been a particular moment when I knew I needed to change my life, but I don't know when it was. The desire for change is like a tiny pebble in a shoe, imperceptible at first but grinding away until it becomes the only thing you notice.

It was not that my existence was miserable; as I entered what I assumed would be the middle years of my life, I had meaningful work and a good man who embellished my existence with such late-twentieth-century emblems of arrival as the loft in Chelsea, the orchestra seats, the signed Miró painting, the vacations on the isles of Nevis and Antigua.

It was more than a reasonable life, it was an enviable one. Yet I was distanced from it. It was his life; it never seemed like mine, a sense that gave rise to a pervasive disappointment I could not shake, though I tried. "What do I want?" I kept asking myself. I could not say for sure. I knew only that I sorely needed something I did not have.

My instinct was to dismiss the feeling. Like many women, I found it easy to recognize the needs and emotions of others and nearly impossible to recognize my own, even those that involved basics such as appetite. I was nearly forty years old before I could say with certainty that I was hungry, and now, confronted with hunger in another, more amorphous form, I told myself that I was simply spoiled, chronically incapable of sustaining any sort of alliance. Still I became engulfed in that sorrowing feeling the Portuguese call *saudades*, which is nostalgia for something that never was.

Then work brought me to Los Angeles, where persimmons grow, where streets are coated in pale blue blooms fallen from the jacaranda trees, where light is softer and brighter than light anywhere else.

I was there to report a piece on the Whitewater figure Susan McDougal, who was doing hard time in a Los Angeles jail, where I visited her each afternoon. At the end of each visit, it pained me that I was free to go and she wasn't. At the same time, as I drove back to my hotel, heading west on the Santa Monica Freeway, the sheer speed, boundless sky, and setting sun reflecting on puffs of pink and golden clouds filled me with appreciation for being free and overwhelmed me with gratitude and wonder.

What would I be like on my own? Would I be reading a book, cat in my lap, sipping tea? Or would that genteel scenario give way to staring into a 5x magnifying mirror, bemoaning the fine lines and wrinkles that were ostensible deal breakers in locating a new life, a new man? But then, I wasn't hungering for a man. I was hungering for communion with myself.

I despised the idea of running away. How could I leave a man who had only been good to me? If I could have convinced myself I *had* to leave, I could have been exempt from responsibility. Yet saying I *wanted* to leave was another matter, a conscious, willful choice to place my own well-being and needs over those of someone else, an act brimming with the enlightened self-assertion praised in men and scorned in women.

Of all the qualities I admire, none matters more to me than courage, and I kept telling myself that I needed the courage to remake my life, whether or not I wanted to.

I started picturing a white room, a room that contained no history, a room devoid of posters from places I would just as soon not have visited, no paintings etched on glass that I should not have bought—a place where the past could be sloughed off.

We get what we need, and soon that white room materialized. It was on the beach, where I could gaze out my window and see before me only sand and sea and sky, where I could nourish a small garden of Mexican bush sage and Iceberg roses, and where the sunset turned the benign blue sky to ferocious golds and purples.

"No one turns their life upside down to look at a sunset," the man I'd lived with said to me. But what I had done was not frivolous. This nearness to the natural world was an antidote to my abiding disappointment. Day by day, it soothed me, it strengthened me, until it had redeemed my spirit, my sense of hope. I did what I needed to do—having come to understand that in this, our only life, our primary obligation is to respond to those needs that are as basic as oxygen, as fundamental as air.

Blame It on the *Bossanova*

Mary South

Several years ago I had notions of myself that I wore like clothes: I was a book editor. Thirty-nine. Single. Relatively successful. Stable. Secure.

Not unhappy.

Double negatives gnaw at an editor, though. "Not unhappy" became increasingly not acceptable. As the walls of my office slowly disappeared behind a fleet of fishing vessel photos, I became more and more obsessed with the dream of salty freedom. So after a bad day at work, I did it: I quit my good job, sold my tiny weekend house in Pennsylvania, packed a duffel bag, and put everything else in storage. I then sank every penny from the sale of my home into the *Bossanova*, a forty-foot, thirty-ton steel trawler that I moved aboard without a clue as to how to run it. Nine weeks of seamanship school later, I pulled away from the dock on my very first trip: a journey up the Atlantic coast from Florida to Maine.

The happiness I found at sea, the sense of accomplishment I felt, made it clear that I was more myself, more me, standing at the helm of my little ship than I had ever been sitting in a conference room. And even though the *Bossanova* now spends as much time at the dock as she does at sea, the lessons I learned on her pitching decks continue to color my days.

I can't count the times that someone has heard my story and said, "Oh, someday I'd love to [insert fantasy here]." I'm not able to tell them how to make that happen, but I can offer what I now understand about two of life's great go-for-it clichés.

First: "Do what you love and the money will follow." Unless you happen to love being a stockbroker, this is not necessarily true. I, for instance, abandoned a six-figure job with an expense account, bonus package, full medical and dental benefits, and a 401(k) plan for . . . genteel poverty. (Taking the proceeds of a house sale and putting them all into a forty-foot, thirty-ton steel boat is probably not what Warren Buffett would have advised as an investment strategy.)

I can honestly say, however, that buying the *Bossanova* was the smartest thing I ever did. In the end, my adventure thrilled me in a way that a fat paycheck and job security never could. And I noticed how much less *stuff* I needed to be happy. I stopped compensating myself for my boredom with expensive things I didn't really need and inevitably lost interest in. So by all means, do what you love, but be prepared for that to be its own reward.

No one prizes reckless abandon more than I do, but "carpe diem" is another adage that should never be taken literally. Seize the day if you must, but do so gently and never, ever shake it. All days are not alike, and some of them are just not meant for seizing. Some days you wake up with a headache, a dentist's appointment, and a long to-do list. But that's okay. Seize tomorrow instead and today follow the path of least resistance—because deciding *not* to seize this particular day is also a form of seizing the day, if you follow my drift.

Actually, the only advice you really need is this: Follow your heart. Just remember that a heart can lead you to some pretty unexpected places. For instance, I set off to navigate the Eastern Seaboard. But I also wound up falling in love, working as a dock master, and writing a book.

None of these were ports I had planned on visiting, but I am who I am because of them.

Adventure comes with no guarantees or promises. Risk and reward are conjoined twins—and that's why my favorite piece of advice needs translation but no disclaimers: *Fortes fortuna juvat.* "Fortune favors the brave," the ancient Roman dramatist Terence declared. In other words, there are many good reasons not to toss your life up in the air and see how it lands. Just don't let fear be one of them.

Lesson Learned

Nanette Terrenal

After nearly two decades in the fashion business, I thought nothing could surprise me—until the day I toured the Guatemalan manufacturing plant that made accessories for the company I worked for. Just about every one of the dozens of factory workers was a child. A very young child. "Let me introduce you to our best one," said the man guiding me through the plant. A ten-year-old boy stood before me smiling proudly, stretching out his small hand.

And then it hit me. *What am I doing?* I realized that in a way I had helped create this shocking scene. Even after I returned to New York City, the question nagged me. Over time I stopped caring about my job. Doing deals was thrilling, but once the dotted lines were signed, the fun was over for me. I wasn't making anything other than money.

I wasn't making a difference. In the evenings I'd sit on my couch wondering why I couldn't be happy with a job other people would kill for.

I endured this confusion for a year before I drummed up the courage to quit. What allowed me to walk away was finally figuring out that my distress was a sign that it was time for me to move on. For a while I worried about what my friends would think. Would they have lunch with me after I had given up my power-player post? I realized, of course, that real friends would and the others would fade away, and that was okay.

So I headed back to my hometown, Los Angeles, where I moved in with my sister-in-law and floundered for months. I was thirty-seven and single and didn't have many expenses, so I could afford to experiment. I wound up taking a job at a small nonprofit agency dedicated to teaching traffic safety to schoolchildren. I was making less than half my old salary, but the job helped me discover that what I really wanted to do was teach. Four years later I started working on my master's degree in education, and now I teach fifth grade at one of the many troubled schools in Los Angeles.

The funny thing is that I left the fashion industry because I wanted to simplify my life, but now I work harder than I ever have. And I love it. It's amazing how when I didn't like what I was doing, the money I made never seemed to be enough. I'd go out and buy and buy and buy, and I'd fill my house with things. The trouble with that is that what you buy doesn't change the fact that you still don't like the way you're spending your life. Now I make even less than what I earned at the nonprofit, and my friends joke that I'm one of the few Americans on a decelerating pay scale. I may not be able to get the $150 pair of shoes I once would have bought without hesitation, or indulge in weekly manicures, but I do wake up every morning and go to a job where I know I am valuable, where I am happy, where I know I am making a difference in my life and in others'. These days, when I ask myself, *What am I doing?* I know the answer.

Swan's Way

Katherine B. Weissman

I'm almost sixty, and not a sylph. I have injury-prone feet, a thickish middle I camouflage with a sweater around my hips, and a brain that often can't keep up with the combinations of steps I'm handed. But for twenty-five years, I've been putting in regular time at the ballet barre, dressed in a stretched-out unitard, baggy shorts or a gauzy skirt, and a sleeveless men's T-shirt, accessorized with an elastic knee bandage. I pick my spot, scrape back my hair, and prepare to sweat. (A towel and a water bottle are never far away.)

Those ninety minutes three times a week are the spine of my life, a ritual as hard and satisfying as any I've ever known. They've helped see me through my mother's death, my divorce, and 9/11 (in class the next day, the pianist played "The Star-Spangled Banner," and we wept).

I took ballet when I was young, and frankly, fat, but gave it up, as girls do, when it became clear that my talent was not equal to my rapture. Then, in my thirties, I fell in love all over again. I hadn't retained much except a vague memory of the five positions of the feet. I didn't have to strive for "beginner's mind." I *was* a beginner.

My attitude, however, was entirely too grown-up—by which I mean cerebral, unspontaneous, and a bit grim. I had the school-ingrained habit of pouring data into my brain, waiting until it was "cooked," then applying it (in this case, to my body, where it would be swirled a little, like cake frosting). Now I realize that the process of learning to dance is considerably more subtle: My physical self seems to acquire knowledge on its own, doing a grand jeté right over my reluctant and analytic mind. It sounds a little schizoid, but I don't *always* know what I know. The more I can trust my body, the better things go.

Things don't always go well, that's for sure. Ballet isn't safe. It is physically unnatural (your hips and feet turn out; you arrange your fingers just so; you move with the hauteur of a denizen of Louis XIV's court, which is where the art was perfected), and it is psychologically exposed (every class is a performance, sort of). The studio is a minefield: I've landed on my butt while attempting a grand plié, collided with another student because I was going the wrong way, blanked totally on the step I was supposed to do next.

Yet I persist, as hooked on dance as the doomed heroine of my favorite movie, *The Red Shoes*. I bring CDs on vacation so I can practice in hotel rooms. My first question after a recent surgery was "When can I go back to class?" During a year in Israel, I braved class with Russians speaking Hebrew; not understanding the words, I got by on pictures. (It is heartening that in a warlike and divided world, ballet survives as an international language.)

Obsession loves company, and adult ballet students, especially older ones, socialize like crazy. We form coteries as we stretch before class or in the humid euphoria of the dressing room afterward, chatting and complaining and comparing notes about teachers, and somehow this coalesces into intimacy. In fact, most of the good friends I've made in the past ten or fifteen years are women I met in class. There is something about the common passion, the shared risk, the revealed and imperfect bodies that bonds us like soldiers—or nuns.

Once the music begins, however, I work alone, even if the room is so crowded that my neighbor's pink slipper on the barre is nudging my hand. Class only appears to be a communal activity; it is actually a kind of meditation, a time and space I claim to focus on feeling centered, physically and mentally. Sure, there is criticism and, less frequently, praise, but learning ballet is a surprisingly private affair. It has taught me not only to hold an arabesque but to maintain an inner grace—drawing on a psychological or spiritual core, a place of honesty and strength. You have to give your heart to dancing; otherwise, you're just going through the motions.

No wonder I'm seduced: Where else would I get to exercise my imagination as well as my body? I envision feathers, tulle, and satin shoes while I'm actually wrapped in layers of Lycra, wool, and ragged cotton. Sometimes—often—I grimace and panic, look wildly about as I totter and flail. But if, during class, just once I find my balance—perched on one leg, arms held high—I am suddenly the remote, powerful, glamorous creature I always dreamed, in my girlish reveries, of becoming: fusing sex with art, soaring into the ineffable, swan *and* woman. Ballet transforms and uplifts. Through it, I take flight.

Are You Listening to Your Life?

Parker J. Palmer

It can take a long time to become yourself. I was in my early thirties when I first began to question my calling, teaching at a university and doing it reasonably well. But I felt stifled by the confines of academic life. A small voice inside was calling me toward something unknown and risky, yet more congruent with my own truth. I couldn't tell, however, whether the voice was trustworthy, whether this truer life I sensed stirring within me was real or within reach.

Then I ran across the old Quaker saying "Let your life speak." I found the words encouraging, and I thought I understood what they meant: Let the loftiest truths and values guide you. Live up to those demanding standards in everything you do. I believed I was being exhorted to live a life of high purpose, as did Martin Luther King Jr., Rosa Parks, and Mahatma Gandhi.

Clinging fearfully to my academic job even though it was a bad fit, I tried to teach the way I imagined my heroes would. The results were rarely admirable, often laughable, and sometimes grotesque, as when I caught myself preaching to students instead of teaching them. I had simply found a "noble" way to live a false life, imitating my heroes instead of listening to my heart. Vocation, the way I was seeking it, had become a grim act of will.

Today, some thirty years later, I've found deep joy in my vocation as a writer, traveling teacher, and activist. And "Let your life speak" means something different to me now. Vocation, I've learned, doesn't come from willfulness. It comes from listening. That insight is hidden in the word *vocation* itself, which is rooted in the Latin word for voice. Before I tell my life what I want to do with it, I must listen for what my life wants to do with me.

I've come to understand vocation not as a goal to be achieved but as a gift to be received—the treasure of true self I already possess. Vocation doesn't come from a voice "out there" calling me to become something I'm not. It comes from a voice "in here" calling me to be the person I was born to be.

Accepting this birthright gift of self turns out to be even more demanding than attempting to become someone else. I've sometimes responded to that demand by ignoring the gift or hiding it or fleeing from it, and I don't think I'm alone. An old Hasidic tale reveals both the universal tendency to want to be someone else and the importance of becoming one's self: Rabbi Zusya, when he was an old man, said, "In the coming world, they will not ask me, 'Why were you not Moses?' They will ask me, 'Why were you not Zusya?'"

When we lose track of our true self, how can we pick up the trail? Our lives speak through our actions and reactions, our intuitions and instincts, our feelings and bodily states, perhaps more profoundly than through words. If we can learn to read our own responses, we'll receive the guidance we need to live more authentic lives. The soul speaks only under quiet, inviting, and safe conditions. If we take some time to sit silently listening, the soul will tell us the truth about ourselves—the full, messy truth. An often ignored dimension of the quest for wholeness is the need to embrace what we dislike about ourselves as well as what we're proud of, our liabilities as well as our strengths.

We can learn as much about who we are from our limits as from our potentials. For years I thought that becoming a college president was the right thing to do with my life, despite the fact that I'm too thin-skinned for the job. But when I embraced this limitation and found work where thin skin is an asset, the fact that I'd never become a college president felt like a homecoming, a return to my true self, full of peace and joy.

We can move toward such homecomings by seeking clues to vocation in childhood memories. When I was a boy, I spent hours putting together little books on how airplanes fly. For a long time I thought that meant I wanted to be a pilot. But a few years ago, I saw that what I'd really wanted all along was to write books.

Our highest calling is to grow into our own authentic selfhood, whether or not it conforms to some image of what others think we ought to be. In doing so, we find not only the joy that every human being seeks but also our path of authentic service in the world. True vocation joins self and service, says theologian Frederick Buechner, who defines vocation as "the place where your deep gladness meets the world's deep need."

The world's deep needs are met daily not only by caring doctors and inspiring teachers but by good parents, good plumbers, good hairdressers, good friends. And as all those people know, the gladness of authentic vocation is always laced with pain. Ask any parent suffering through the travails of her child's teenage years.

But the pain that comes from doing the right job well and the pain that tells us we're on the wrong track are different—and the soul knows the difference. When we're on the wrong track, the soul feels violated and abused and cries out for change. But when we suffer from doing the right job well, the soul still feels fulfilled, because it knows how to take this kind of suffering and use it to make meaning and extend the heart's reach.

This emphasis on self and gladness has nothing to do with selfishness. The Quaker writer Douglas Steere said that the ancient human question "Who am I?" leads inevitably to the equally important question "Whose am I?" since there is not selfhood outside of relationship.

When we answer the "Who am I?" question as honestly as we can, we will be more authentically connected to the community around us and will serve more faithfully the people whose lives we touch—for the gift of self is, finally, the only gift we have to give.

Keeping the Flame

Patti Smith

When I was young, everything seemed so simple. I felt the calling toward art and literature, so I decided I would be a writer and pen a magical book like *Peter Pan* or *Alice in Wonderland*. But no matter how fixed I was on my path, something always drew me away and I tramped unexpected roads with great twists and turns. And what I learned is that we are all Pinocchio: We begin our life, waving to our mother and father with our schoolbooks in hand, hoping to do well. But we are turned this way and that. We make mistakes, we move from our course, we falter, flounder, and may suffer remorse, rebellion, or a sense of defeat. We seem to lose our way. But no matter! If we keep our little flame alive, our first feeling of enthusiasm of who we are, without the influence or intervention of others, we will prevail.

And like Pinocchio, despite all his transgressions, find the courage to reunite with our little flame and be rewarded. And the reward is this: We become ourselves.

In my life I have made many mistakes. Sometimes I was careless and inconsiderate of others. Fate drew me to singing and performing around the world, and yet this was not what I dreamed for myself—sometimes I felt it took me from my true path, that of the writer. But I found performing brought me closer to people. It gave me an opportunity to travel, to explore, to communicate, and to concern myself with my fellow man.

In 1979 I gave up my life in the arena of rock 'n' roll to marry and raise a family, another divergence from my pursuit as a solitary artist. But through my family I learned the final lesson of Pinocchio—what it is like to be human. And always through everything, through sacrifice and success, I have tried to stay close to my little flame, reminding me who I am.

The cricket tells Pinocchio, "Always let your conscience be your guide." These words, by a small, insignificant insect, give us all we need. The best person to tell you who you are, what you should be, is ultimately yourself.

Contributors

Helena Andrews, author of the memoir-in-essays *Bitch Is the New Black*, is a columnist based in Washington, D.C.

Natalie Baszile holds an M.A. in Afro-American Studies from UCLA and an M.F.A. from Warren Wilson College's M.F.A. Program for Writers, where she was a Holden Minority Scholar. She is a member of the San Francisco Writers' Grotto and lives in the Bay Area.

Martha Beck, Ph.D., is a life coach whose most recent book, *The Martha Beck Collection: Essays for Creating Your Right Life, Volume 1,* is an anthology of her work from *O, The Oprah Magazine*, where she's been a columnist since 2001. Beck's other books include *Leaving the Saints,*

Finding Your Own North Star, The Joy Diet, Steering by Starlight, and *Finding Your Way in a Wild New World.*

Robin Black is the award-winning author of the story collection *If I Loved You, I Would Tell You This*; the novel *Life Drawing*; and the forthcoming *Crash Course: 52 Essays from Where Writing and Life Collide.* She lives with her family in Philadelphia.

Alain de Botton cofounded the School of Life in London and writes essayistic books—on subjects ranging from travel to architecture—that have been described as a "philosophy of everyday life."

Valorie Burton, bestselling author and certified personal and executive coach, has written nine books on personal development, including *Successful Women Think Differently* and *Happy Women Live Better.*

Lorene Cary is the author of *Black Ice*, a memoir; a book on the Underground Railroad for young readers; and three novels, including *The Price of a Child* and *If Sons, Then Heirs.*

Mallika Chopra founded Intent.com as an online destination for turning intentions into tangible actions. She is the author of *Living with Intent: My Somewhat Messy Journey to Purpose, Peace, and Joy.*

Michael Cunningham is the author of the novels *A Home at the End of the World, Flesh and Blood, The Hours* (winner of the Pen/Faulkner Award and Pulitzer Prize), *The Snow Queen, Specimen Days,* and *By Nightfall,* as well as the nonfiction book *Land's End: A Walk in Provincetown.* His new book is *A Wild Swan and Other Tales* (illustrated by Yuko Shimizu). He lives in New York and teaches at Yale University.

Edwidge Danticat is the author of several works of fiction (*Breath, Eyes, Memory; Krik? Krak!; The Farming of Bones; The Dew Breaker;* and *Claire of the Sea Light*), numerous works of nonfiction (*Brother, I'm Dying; After the Dance: A Walk Through Carnival in Jacmel, Haiti;* and *Create Dangerously: The Immigrant Artist at Work*), as well as several picture books and novels for young adults. Danticat was a 2009 MacArthur Foundation Fellow.

Anne Dranitsaris, Ph.D., has worked as a clinical psychotherapist for more than thirty years; she specializes in the fields of personal and professional growth.

Mark Epstein, M.D., a psychiatrist in private practice in New York City, is the author of several books about the nexus of Buddhism and psychotherapy, including *Thoughts Without a Thinker, Going to Pieces Without Falling Apart,* and *The Trauma of Everyday Life.*

Suzanne Finnamore is a bestselling novelist and the author of *Split: A Memoir of Divorce.* She lives with her husband and three children in North Carolina.

Bonnie Friedman divides her time between Brooklyn, New York, and Denton, Texas, where she teaches creative writing at the University of North Texas. She is the author of *Surrendering Oz: A Life in Essays* and *Writing Past Dark: Envy, Fear, Distraction, and Other Dilemmas in the Writer's Life.*

Elizabeth Gilbert has written seven books of fiction and nonfiction. Her memoir *Eat, Pray, Love* sold over ten million copies, and her latest novel, *The Signature of All*

Things, was named a best book of the year by *Time, The New York Times,* and *The Washington Post.*

Barbara Graham, an award-winning journalist, writes extensively about psychology and spirituality. Her most recent book was *The New York Times* bestselling *Eye of My Heart.*

Kathryn Harrison has written for *The New York Times Book Review, The New Yorker, Harper's Magazine,* and *Vogue,* among others, and is the author of fourteen books.

Amy Hempel's celebrated short fiction can be found in *The Collected Stories of Amy Hempel.* Her latest work, *The Hand That Feeds You,* is a novel cowritten with Jill Ciment and published under the name A. J. Rich.

Elizabeth Kaye is a ballet historian and the author of seven books, most recently two e-books: *Lifeboat No. 8: An Untold Tale of Love, Loss, and Surviving the Titanic* and *Sleeping with Famous Men: Memories of an Unconventional Love Life,* an anthology of her magazine pieces. She lives in Los Angeles.

Jennifer Krause, author of *The Answer: Making Sense of Life, One Question at a Time*, was the first woman to serve as High Holidays rabbi at Manhattan's 92Y in its 140-year history. She lives in New York City.

Laura Munson, founder of the Haven Writing Retreats in Montana, is the author of *This Is Not the Story You Think It Is . . .*

Parker J. Palmer, Ph.D., is the author of nine books—including the bestselling *Healing the Heart of Democracy*, *The Courage to Teach*, and *Let Your Life Speak*. The recipient of a variety of national awards and twelve honorary doctorates, he is also founder and senior partner of the Center for Courage & Renewal.

Ellen Roth is a certified sign language interpreter as well as a nutritional and spiritual counselor.

Danzy Senna wrote the bestselling novel *Caucasia*, as well as the novel *Symptomatic*, the memoir *Where Did You Sleep Last Night? A Personal History*, and a story collection, *You Are Free*. A recipient of the Whiting

Award, she lives in Los Angeles with her husband and children.

Patti Smith is a performer, author, and visual artist. Her memoir, *Just Kids,* was awarded the National Book Award in 2010. She was inducted into the Rock and Roll Hall of Fame, named Commandeur des Arts et des Lettres by the French Republic, and has received Sweden's Polar Award for significant achievements in music. Her new book, published by Knopf, is *M Train.*

Mary South, author of *The Cure for Anything Is Salt Water: How I Threw My Life Overboard and Found Happiness at Sea,* is editor-in-chief of the boating magazine *Soundings.*

Nanette Terrenal is an elementary school principal in Los Angeles, where she continues to pursue her purpose: providing educational opportunities to low-income and immigrant children.

Eliza Thomas resides in Montpelier, Vermont, where she works as a piano teacher and accompanist. She hopes someday to write a mystery novel with musical overtones.

Katherine B. Weissman, a New York City-based writer and editor, is currently working on a fantasy novel for older adults.

Paige Williams is an award-winning writer who teaches at the Missouri School of Journalism. Her narrative nonfiction book *The Dinosaur Artist* is slated to be published in 2016.

Marianne Williamson, a bestselling author and lecturer, has written fourteen books, including *A Return to Love.*

Wini Yunker is the Democratic election commissioner for Jessamine County, Kentucky, and caretaker of a 210-acre tobacco and corn farm. At seventy-nine, she was the oldest person to take the Brave the Blue Challenge, a yearly scouting fund-raiser in Lexington, Kentucky, that involves rappelling from a 410-foot-tall building.